Who Cares?

Who Cares?

Meditations for Lent

Craig Ward

Inspirational Faith

Published by Inspirational Faith

Copyright © 2012 Inspirational Faith

All rights reserved. This publication may not be reproduced, stored in a retrieval system or transmitted, in any form or by any means, electronic mechanical, photocopying, recording or otherwise, without the prior permission of the copyright owner.

All Scripture references are taken from the New International Version 1984

ISBN 978-0-9562559-7-6

inspirationalfaith.net

Who Cares ?

Two opposites defined

Who Cares?

Who gives a stuff about you? I'm not interested; you have needs, so do I.
Others will help surely. Why me? I'm off to Nineveh.
Caring is too costly; no one cares for me. ☹

Who Cares?

I love you. Please share what I have. I've been given to; let me give to you.
I've been there too – it's painful; let me show you someone who can help.
Please let me help; I care and love you deeply. ☺

Contents

The Meditations

Shrove Tuesday	Preparation Day	12
Day 1	Here I come, ready or not	17
Day 2	I'm too busy to care	21
Day 3	Being a caring person	26
Day 4	Being a caring Christian	32
Day 5	God so loved the world	39
Day 6	God caring	44
Day 7	Being alive to God and caring	49
Day 8	Love one another	54
Day 9	Caring for ourselves	59
Day 10	Trusting in God – faith and mountains	64
Day 11	How to ignore the world and get away with it	69
Day 12	The six step care dance – steps to follow	74
Day 13	Dance 1: Listening	79
Day 14	Dance 2: Taking time to know them	84
Day 15	Dance 3: Warning against refusing God	89
Day 16	Dance 4: Release from suffering	94

Day 17	Dance 5: The devil and all that stuff	99
Day 18	Dance 6: Jesus every time	105
Day 19	Dance 7: Have a rest as God did	110
Day 20	Love me ... as this is all there is	115
Day 21	Just who controls me then?	120
Day 22	How to love others from where you are	124
Day 23	How to love others by listening to them	129
Day 24	How to love others – love in a fallen world	134
Day 25	How to love others – living for Jesus	139
Day 26	How to love others – receiving love	144
Day 27	God in a caring world	149
Day 28	Fruits without actions	154
Day 29	Doing the right thing today	160
Day 30	The fruits of worry	165
Day 31	Waiting for the kettle to boil	170
Day 32	Being the bystander	175
Day 33	Is God real or was I mistaken?	181
Day 34	Being obedience	186
Day 35	The onward Christian struggle	191
Day 36	Being busy to care today	196
Day 37	Fearing the unexplainable	201
Day 38	We too can walk on water	206

Day 39	Receiving love and care from others	211
Day 40	Jesus the deliberate king	217
Day 41	Furniture hurling	222
Day 42	Frustration and love	227
Day 43	Worthy to care – a life for Jesus	232
Day 44	The lamb or the vegetarian option	237
Day 45	Jesus dies	242
Day 46	A moment of your time please	247
Day 47	Mmmmmm, tea and chocolate	253

The Meditations

Shrove Tuesday

Preparation Day

Reading: Exodus 12:39

³⁹ With the dough they had brought from Egypt, they baked cakes of unleavened bread. The dough was without yeast because they had been driven out of Egypt and did not have time to prepare food for themselves.

Meditation

In the small hours approaching dawn, we see the rabble tribe of Moses fleeing for their lives into the hostile Egyptian desert. Returning is death, venturing into unmapped desert is folly, yet here they run. Preparation is everything. Just visiting our local shops takes a long checklist: bag, keys, money, plastic cards, shopping list, shopping bag, change for parking, hat, coat, gloves, scarf, let alone all the other things lurking in the bottom of our bags. And all we're buying is a birthday card, not fleeing from our neighbours, yet. Time is endowed as a luxury at our disposal, born in readiness for what may happen, the eventualities of our placid journeys. Not so for a fleeing tribe one starry night – grab it and go now, they're coming.

Jesus too knew people coming to harm him: "Rise, lets us go! Here comes my betrayer" (Matthew 26: 46). Unlike the tribe of Moses, Jesus waits patiently, knowing Judas, who hours before was smiling and laughing as they ate, but now comes with murder in his heart for the Son of Man. The fleeing has ended, here and now God makes His stand, this far and no more. Today, now, God says, "I conclude the fleeing tribes, because I care. No more will my people flee. I will save them in ways they do not know or may never comprehend. Today I the Lord of all have spoken – beware."

Amongst our busyness lives a question: do we care, really honestly care? We don't have to be bothered with everyone's concerns around us. Walking away to us may not matter, but to them it's all that matters. Our lives briefly touch theirs and all the love we give is, "No thanks, I'm busy." We move to the other side of the road and keep walking – "I'm busy, no one minds." Showing we care takes time, our precious time. It's our time to do with as we wish, no conditions attached. Many already give their time freely; for others today's their decision time. Do I care enough to help, or shall I walk on by? I don't have to care. It's in the Bible, others have walked by too.

Our Lenten Journey
No matter if we care, either way we bring to our Lenten journey's beginning our bags of self concern, future hopes, tears endured, joys shared with mingled moments of regret. We too bring Jesus, as we have known and walked with Him. For some the path seems empty: "He's never walked with me, I was alone, always." For others, there's a need to touch Jesus once more. Still others already walk with Him, hand in hand.

Reach out – Jesus is waiting, waiting for our hand. He's very good at reaching out, even in death on His cross reaching out and touching a sinner's hand next to His: "Today you will be with me in paradise." No matter who we are, where we've been, what we've done, Jesus reaches out. We just have to hold His hand; with Jesus promising, "Today you will be with me in paradise," if we just reach out to Him.

47 and a Half Days
Why 47 and a half? This figure comes from adding the eventide feast of the night before the 40 days of Lent, plus all the Sundays and Easter day, making 47 and a half days in total. Over the next 47 and a half days we'll be exploring the 'if's' and 'how's' of do we care for each other. We'll be looking at how

our own needs need not always be our only thoughts; others are important too. And if we sincerely wish to care for them, their needs will also be on our mind.

Caring comes in two versions
Who Cares 1:   Who gives a stuff about you? I'm not interested; you have needs so do I. Others will help surely. Why me? I'm off to Nineveh. Caring is too costly; no one cares for me.
Who Cares 2:   I love you. Please share what I have. I've been given to; let me give to you. I've been there too – it's painful; let me show you someone who can help; please let me help; I care and love you deeply ☺

The Choices of Jesus
Each of us has a choice, just as Jesus gave His disciples choices: "Come follow me…" (Mark 1:17); except we don't have to follow Him. Jesus says to those who do follow, "Go and do likewise." With saying yes we enter on a sometimes frightening, certainly baffling, and at times exhilarating walk with Jesus. Walking with Him, as His disciples quickly found, comes with tasks. The first one is eating – this occupies His disciples' minds quite frequently. Feeding on hillsides, in boats, around Jerusalem, a last supper, on beaches, in hidden rooms, in open fields. Jesus chose very food orientated disciples – bit like us really.

Pancakes, Mmmmmm
Traditionally it used to be that on this night, Shrove Tuesday, all our niceties from our cupboards were eaten to celebrate throughout Lent a chastised abstinence from foodly pleasures. I think the best we manage now is giving up chocolate or Jaffa cakes. Below is a recipe, to quell the fires of pleasure.

Take 4oz of plain flour, an egg of goodly size, ½ pint of milk, and a pinch of salt. Mix together and fry with oil both sides. Add lemons and sugar to taste and eat; not running, but with a friend you'd like to maybe know a little better as the Lenten time unfolds.

Come Follow Me

Jesus says of those who journey with him, "Come to me all who are weary and burdened, and I will give you rest" (Matthew 11:28). If we care enough about ourselves to come to Jesus and accept His rest, how much more should we share with others what we've found? How much should we give, as Jesus gives His care to us?

We don't have to care. Jesus never said you have to perform so many good works to earn your place in heaven. He gives freely the gift of eternal life to those who believe. Just as He gave His time to care whilst walking the planet. Should we too be g ving ourselves in the service of others, just as Jesus gave His life for us?

Prayer

Father, help me see if you will have me give of myself today. Show me where there is a need and help me to meet that need, not in my strength, but in yours, Amen.

Memory verse

John 6:35

Then Jesus declared, "I am the bread of life. He who comes to me will never go hungry, and he who believes in me will never be thirsty."

Action

Invite one friend, who you know well, and share some pancakes with them.

Day 1   Ash Wednesday

Here I come, ready or not

Reading: Isaiah 40:1-8

Comfort for God's People

¹ Comfort, comfort my people, says your God.
² Speak tenderly to Jerusalem, and proclaim to her that her hard service has been completed, that her sin has been paid for, that she has received from the LORD's hand double for all her sins.

³ A voice of one calling: "In the desert prepare the way for the LORD; make straight in the wilderness a highway for our God.
⁴ Every valley shall be raised up, every mountain and hill made low; the rough ground shall become level, the rugged places a plain.
⁵ And the glory of the LORD will be revealed, and all mankind together will see it. For the mouth of the LORD has spoken."

⁶ A voice says, "Cry out." And I said, "What shall I cry?" "All men are like grass, and all their glory is like the flowers of the field.
⁷ The grass withers and the flowers fall, because the breath of the LORD blows on them. Surely the people are grass.
⁸ The grass withers and the flowers fall, but the word of our God stands forever."

Meditation

Our lives sometimes seem lead up to points of, well, which way do we go now? Are we ready for what comes next, or still stumbling around looking for clues? Being prepared is the only option, prepared and waiting for the challenges we know life hurls around, just as we see Jesus waiting for moments. What's important is how we respond in those moments. Miss it and it never comes again.

Isaiah the writer is a city man, an urban dweller, as is sensed from his writings. He's surrounded by Jerusalem, a prosperous town suffering the throws of economic changes, a credit crunch of the 700's BC. Isaiah is writing somewhere between the decline of Israel and the stormy rise in power of the Assyrians. His book presents a God of power, judgement, and salvation – one who comes with vengeance upon those who oppose Him, bringing hope and renewing those who trust in Him. They will soar like eagles (Is.40:31) as the Lord wipes away their tears (Is.25:8). Isaiah writes about a future punctuated by waiting, waiting for events to unfold, for circumstances to crystallise into God's future plans. Central to God's plans are fragile us, you and me, frail yet head strong with all sorts of plans of our own, frequently opposing God and the best He wants for us. God must feel very frustrated most of the time.

Isaiah is a book about prophecies, a book of preparation. It requires readers to consider the enormity of what is about to happen, pointing to a man in time destined to change the planet – Jesus. But it's also about waiting, the thing none of us like to do. When do I want it? NOW! Well of course now – that's our world, by choice or infliction – definitely negative, until you add Jesus.

Waiting, as Jesus knew, is crucial. It underpins everything He does. He acts when the time is right. For instance, just how do you change the world? You get into a boat on a lake in Gennesaret, sit down, and start teaching the crowd on the shore. Only then do you ask Simon, who owns the boat, to set up another fishing trip (Luke 5:1-11). Jesus seizes the right moment. Simon (who later becomes Peter, the rock on which Jesus built His church) leaves everything he owns and follows Him. His brother Andrew had heard about Jesus from a man called John (Jn.1:35-42), and had then told his brother Simon to come and see. John has been preaching in the wilderness, shouting to all who would listen, "The promised one is coming." John sets the scene, Andrew makes the connection, but Jesus waits for the moment.

Time is both an instant and a commodity. Expressed at the right time, the action works, but wait too long and both the moment and commodity are wasted. Jesus shows in waiting, how he observes patience and concern for what's about to occur: Simon leaving everything and following Him. Simon, like many fishermen, had fished the same area since a boy, this was his life. Jesus changes lives by inviting people to follow Him. But Jesus knows there is a cost. The cost is 'everything' to follow him, no holding back. Jesus knows too that asking everything of frail humanity is sometimes asking too much. No matter how much we might say, "Yes of course you can have everything," Jesus knows us much too well, knowing that, just like Simon, we get it wrong, want it all back again, and will on occasions wriggle to rid ourselves of the yoke of following Jesus.

Only someone who cares deeply for us without reserve waits for us. Ever had that meeting where the other person's late? How long should I wait before I go? Eventually we have to go. Not so with Jesus. He is that person, constantly waiting for us to remember the meeting and decide to turn up. Time for him is a commodity used in waiting for us to arrive at the meeting. Sometimes we don't even realise it's a fixed appointment, and it seems as if by accident we find Jesus and come to know Him. Jesus waited for the right time. John set the scene, Andrew made the connection, but Jesus waited for the moment.

Caring is about waiting for moments, moments when others are ready for care. Care cannot be imposed. Try imposing it and see what happens. It just doesn't work. It also means being ready for when we ourselves need caring for, seeing how far we've gone, and accepting that now we need help ourselves. Care too is responding to the passing glance from someone that says, "I'm hurting and I don't know how to say it 'cause it's just too embarrassing to ask for help."

Do we have time to care? Jesus does. What about us?

Prayer

Jesus, thank you for your patience in my life, and thank you that you care enough for me to wait for me, no matter how long it takes. Help me to wait for those I care for, helping me to share with them the same care I receive from you. Teach me Lord how you would have me care, what you would have me learn from my caring, and help me to be the carer you would have me be. In Jesus' name Amen.

Memory verse

Mark 1: 17

[17] "Come, follow me," Jesus said, "and I will make you fishers of men."

Action

Smile and say, "Hello, how are you?" to people you meet, work with, socialise with, or would like to know better, today. Remember that we must be sincere in our actions, respecting the privacy of those around us. If they don't smile back or return our compliment, a silent prayer thanking God for them may be more appropriate than continued attempts at conversation.

Day 2

I'm too busy to care

Reading: Luke 14:15-24

The Parable of the Great Banquet

[15] When one of those at the table with him heard this, he said to Jesus, "Blessed is the man who will eat at the feast in the kingdom of God." [16] Jesus replied: "A certain man was preparing a great banquet and invited many guests. [17] At the time of the banquet he sent his servant to tell those who had been invited, 'Come, for everything is now ready.' [18] "But they all alike began to make excuses. The first said, 'I have just bought a field, and I must go and see it. Please excuse me.' [19] "Another said, 'I have just bought five yoke of oxen, and I'm on my way to try them out. Please excuse me.' [20] "Still another said, 'I just got married, so I can't come.' [21] "The servant came back and reported this to his master. Then the owner of the house became angry and ordered his servant, 'Go out quickly into the streets and alleys of the town and bring in the poor, the crippled, the blind and the lame.' [22] "'Sir,' the servant said, 'what you ordered has been done, but there is still room.' [23] "Then the master told his servant, 'Go out to the roads and country lanes and make them come in, so that my house will be full. [24] I tell you, not one of those men who were invited will get a taste of my banquet.'"

Meditation

Are we too busy to care, or are we just distracted? Whatever our reasons, they're only reasons if we can justify them. Without such justification, they remain excuses, naked in their evidence of our lack of care. Piercing these requires us to see them as they are, no more than preventers, 'stops' as to why we should not care.

Luke 14 portrays a rather hapless group of characters with some of the most unfortunate party excuses ever. The story unfolds with three seemingly good reasons why the party goers can't attend: property purchases, cutting-edge farming animals, and the newly-weds – "Well sorry, I'm busy, honest." We can't always be there, and that's the point of the passage. And oh, I'm sorry, almost forgot: if you wish to opt out of the Kingdom of God, you don't have to RSVP the invite, or go to the party – your choice, but then you're not in heaven. It is 'the' warning parable over being invited into God's Kingdom and our finding reasons not to come. The result: missing out on the gleaming paradise with Jesus. We don't have to come, honestly.

Excuses, good, bad or ugly, appear quite regularly in our lives: "Sorry, I'm too busy to visit," "Sorry I'm too tired for that," "Sorry, I'm ... well, sorry." Let's call it 'the Excuse'. The Excuse exists in every question mankind ever asked – it may not always get used, but it's there waiting. Eve managed one with a bit of help from a snake; David had a good one over Uriah's death: "...war is war..." Sorry he's dead (2 Samuel 11:25); Peter managed three (Matthew 26:69-75). When it comes to questions about do I care, there comes too the momentary Excuse option, no matter who's asking. Do I care? Why should I care what happens? Do I want to care about them enough to help them out?

So why the Excuse? It's our nature – being human, flawed, we consider us first. For some there's an instant move to, "What can I do for them". However, in the fractionary moment, the Excuse option is open. There is nothing wrong with this. It enables us to see whether we need to do something or not. Perhaps we don't know what to do, don't have the experience, need a break, want them to try first, or really don't care what happens. Underpinning these are layers of care we've received, colouring our experience of care at another's hand – what we thought of them, what they did to us, and why we thought they did it. Where these come from, it's hard to tell. Are they self concerned motives? "What will others think if I don't or do?" "I couldn't ..., they're just too ..." Are these an Excuse, or have we found a reason not to care?

One of the commands given to Israel is to "...love your neighbour as yourself" (Leviticus 19:18), a law with consequences. Jesus receives this reply from a Jewish lawyer asking how he can inherit eternal life. Jesus responds with the Good Samaritan parable (Luke 10:25-37) in which two characters definitely exercise the Excuse, passing by, all too busy to care. The other traveller in the Good Samaritan story presents another challenge.

The Jews at the time disliked Samaritans. The Jews and the Samaritans were two neighbouring nations, both worshipping God. National tensions were high, initially over allegations of Samaritan corruption as they mixed with foreigners, and later over rebuilding the temple in Jerusalem around 520 BC (Ezra 4:2). Over 500 years later the feud still raged.

The challenge presented by the Good Samaritan parable is this: would we stop and help? Of course we would – daft question. But do we? In 1973 Darley and Batson conducted some research entitled 'From Jerusalem to Jericho: A study of Situational and Dispositional Variables in Helping Behaviour' (JPSP, 1973, 27:100-108). Using seminary students, they asked them either to prepare a talk on the Good Samaritan or one about seminary jobs. The researchers asked the students to complete a personality questionnaire, and then go over to another building, varying the urgency to arrive there. Part way between the two buildings, on the ground, and clearly in need of help, lay the decoy. Overall, 40% offered the 'victim' help. If the students were hurrying, this dropped to 10%, rising to 63% for those not rushing. There was no difference in the helping behaviour of students going to talk about the Good Samaritan or seminary jobs.

Being in a hurry doesn't prevent us from helping. It just narrows down our ability to accurately assess the needs of the victim. The hurrying students reported they did not always perceive the need to intervene. The researchers concluded, preaching a sermon on the Good Samaritan does, "...not increase helping behaviour..." The hurrying person presented with a needy situation is placed in conflict – a conflict between having to be somewhere else and stopping to care for someone in need.

And for us, we may not be always hurrying, but other distractions come along. Our caring gets interrupted, through schedules, choices, and chores we have to do. These claim our attention and importance, but often, when they fade, we are left asking ourselves why we did not show care. Our interruptions, those missed moments, are not without regret.

Sometimes we are too busy, and being busy is OK, if we don't let our busyness become our Excuse. On the whole, the students rushing to their talks wished to show compassion, but their "Sorry" got there first. Jesus is not asking for perfect caring, He only asks that we do care.

Caring is not easy. Not everyone loves and cares in the same way. We're different, because that's how God designed us. He would have it no other way. It's not an easy task, as Jesus knows, to care. He left us the greatest gift He could, the gift of the Holy Spirit, who encourages and prompts us in our busyness, to see whether we should cross the room and show our care.

In all of what today offers us, inside there is a cry, the cry of Jesus asking, "Do you care?" Is that cry being stifled, is the Excuse option being used, or are we replying: "Show me how I can."

Prayer

Father, today, right now, help me to see what care can do in another life. Show me what stops me caring for others in the same way that you cared for this world through Jesus. Help me, with your Holy Spirit, to be your caring hands to those around me. Amen.

Memory verse

Matthew 10:16

I am sending you out like sheep among wolves. Therefore be as shrewd as snakes and as innocent as doves.

Action

Look at your neighbourhood, the people around you. What do you think they may need help with? Go and see if they do need help. Help can just be chatting or passing the time of day, making sure they're ok.

Day 3

Being a caring person

Reading: Joshua 6:1-25

¹ Now the gates of Jericho were securely barred because of the Israelites. No one went out and no one came in. ² Then the LORD said to Joshua, "See, I have delivered Jericho into your hands, along with its king and its fighting men. ³ March around the city once with all the armed men. Do this for six days. ⁴ Have seven priests carry trumpets of rams' horns in front of the ark. On the seventh day, march around the city seven times, with the priests blowing the trumpets. ⁵ When you hear them sound a long blast on the trumpets, have the whole army give a loud shout; then the wall of the city will collapse and the army will go up, everyone straight in."

⁶ So Joshua son of Nun called the priests and said to them, "Take up the ark of the covenant of the LORD and have seven priests carry trumpets in front of it." ⁷ And he ordered the army, "Advance! March around the city, with an armed guard going ahead of the ark of the LORD."

⁸ When Joshua had spoken to the people, the seven priests carrying the seven trumpets before the LORD went forward, blowing their trumpets, and the ark of the LORD's covenant followed them. ⁹ The armed guard marched ahead of the priests who blew the trumpets, and the rear guard followed the ark. All this time the trumpets were sounding. ¹⁰ But Joshua had commanded the army, "Do not give a war cry, do not raise your voices, do not say a word until the day I tell you to shout. Then shout!" ¹¹ So he had the ark of the LORD carried around the city, circling it once. Then the army returned to camp and spent the night there.

¹² Joshua got up early the next morning and the priests took up the ark of the LORD. ¹³ The seven priests carrying the seven trumpets went forward, marching before the ark of the LORD and blowing the trumpets. The armed

men went ahead of them and the rear guard followed the ark of the LORD, while the trumpets kept sounding. [14] So on the second day they marched around the city once and returned to the camp. They did this for six days.

[15] On the seventh day, they got up at daybreak and marched around the city seven times in the same manner, except that on that day they circled the city seven times. [16] The seventh time around, when the priests sounded the trumpet blast, Joshua commanded the army, "Shout! For the LORD has given you the city! [17] The city and all that is in it are to be devoted[a] to the LORD. Only Rahab the prostitute and all who are with her in her house shall be spared, because she hid the spies we sent. [18] But keep away from the devoted things, so that you will not bring about your own destruction by taking any of them. Otherwise you will make the camp of Israel liable to destruction and bring trouble on it. [19] All the silver and gold and the articles of bronze and iron are sacred to the LORD and must go into his treasury."

[20] When the trumpets sounded, the army shouted, and at the sound of the trumpet, when the men gave a loud shout, the wall collapsed; so everyone charged straight in, and they took the city. [21] They devoted the city to the LORD and destroyed with the sword every living thing in it—men and women, young and old, cattle, sheep and donkeys.

[22] Joshua said to the two men who had spied out the land, "Go into the prostitute's house and bring her out and all who belong to her, in accordance with your oath to her." [23] So the young men who had done the spying went in and brought out Rahab, her father and mother, her brothers and sisters and all who belonged to her. They brought out her entire family and put them in a place outside the camp of Israel.

[24] Then they burned the whole city and everything in it, but they put the silver and gold and the articles of bronze and iron into the treasury of the LORD's house. [25] But Joshua spared Rahab the prostitute, with her family and all who belonged to her, because she hid the men Joshua had sent as spies to Jericho—and she lives among the Israelites to this day.

Meditation

We all have views, they might not be good views, but they're ours.

When these are deeply held, changing them is like changing our inmost being – impossible, almost.

Changing derives from two extremes: changing because we ought to, or changing because we accept personal responsibility for ourselves. Changes affect not only our lives, but the situation, and the lives of those around us. For example, the situation may be changed from being impossible to merely difficult, and those around us may be changed to see the world differently, pausing to sense reality, where they are in the world and their role within it. Sometimes circumstances exists where there is no change, irrespective of all the possibilities. There is no movement, no change of heart – just stillness and acceptance of overwhelming hopelessness. These are times when things are just too much, times when there are too many things to deal with, too many variables to manage; times when it's easier to turn and walk away. And then there's Jesus in the midst of all of this asking us to stay a little longer. Jesus cares for us, no matter what we say or do (and no matter how many times we say or do them). He asks us (Luke 10:37) to go and do the same, to care, just care.

At times it may seem impossible to meet their needs. It may be beyond what I can manage. For me it often is. But Jesus asks me to do the same as He does – to just care. Like Rahab in Joshua 6, we need only to see how we can respond to the need around us. She saw a need, partly her own and partly those of the spies, and responded with kindness and care. It gets easier the more we show how much we care.

Joshua 6 is a bewildering story of visiting places and making new friends (if you don't mind having to remodel a burnt out town). The book of Joshua depicts a brave yet near leaderless nomadic tribe emerging from the desert (Moses is dead and Joshua's still working it out). 'Israel' (still only a tribe) has crossed the muddy Jordan, entered the promised land, and stands poised to claim it as their own. Throughout Joshua's book we see discrete responses to differing Israelite needs. First up is Rahab the prostitute.

We known she is a prostitute, but we also discover she loves her family deeply. What else could possibly motivate her into hiding two spies intent on destroying the life she's built and convincing her to deceive her own people.

Already God is working miracles in her life, gently changing her inner being. Her faith in the Israelite God grows through her encounter with the spies. This God of theirs performs wonders she could not have imagined. She knows the temperature of her own country (Joshua 2:9). Fear of this God possesses them all. To her, these spies present not only a way out of her current life (prostitutes did not command great respect in Jericho society). They come to share with her the love of which her own nation is barren. They share with her a relationship with a loving God.

There is no accident in Rahab's actions. She is part of God's plan in securing the land for his people. God is already showing her His love and care. Her response is to show the same 'kindness' she has received. The Hebrew word here is 'hesed' better translated as loyalty, love, or showing intimacy (there is a certain irony in a prostitute to showing this sort of intimacy towards a hostile force). As Jericho falls, Rahab's life changes, from a hired lover to one loved by a caring God. Her actions show how, in the midst of dire need, our God has prepared the way. Rahab claims she personally 'knows' (in Hebrew 'yada', meaning to ascertain by seeing) what God has done. She certainly knew (as Joshua 2:8-11 portrays) of a God who conquers all before Him. She saw in the faces of her neighbours the fear of a God they had never met. What is her response? She extends her concern to the neighbour she has never met.

What would our actions have been? A man without actions is like the fisherman by the pond waiting for the fish to climb out and lay on the bank for him. Likewise with caring: we can go and do something, or we can buy ourselves a comfy chair and theorise. Of course we can always wait for the fish to climb out and cook themselves.

Imagine a different Joshua story, one in which Rahab misses helping the spies. James 2:25 would read differently. No longer would we read, "In the same way, was not Rahab the prostitute considered righteous for what she did when she gave lodging to the spies and sent them off in a different direction." Rahab would be slain with the rest of Jericho. Nothing would have stopped God capturing the place. Her life would not have been spared as it was when she showed compassion for a foreign God and his emissaries.

Caring, as Rahab shows, is not a chore. It can be hard sometimes and full of frustration, but it's where God wants us at that moment. God wanted Rahab at home waiting for His spies to turn up. Just so she could help them. That was her act of caring. She cared, and so we have James 2:25.

Is it easy to be a caring person? Honestly, caring for others is frequently hard and thankless. The easy bit's acknowledging we should care. The hard bit's actually doing the caring. Jesus never said it was going to be easy. We may often misunderstand, or get it wrong – it's part of caring. This is the even harder part: working out how to care, what to say or do, when to offer help. And when should we just be there, doing nothing, sitting with them – the quiet part of caring?

Jesus' own ideas of caring may come as a surprise: "If you, though you are evil, know how to give good gifts to your children, how much more will your Father in heaven give good gifts to those who ask him?" (Matthew 7:11). It is not hard to be a caring person in these terms. We know this, yet it may take us some time to get there. But we know what we should do, because we've been on the experiencing end of being cared for.

In all likelihood, Rahab's original intentions were of saving her own skin, and that of her family. She knew the Jews were coming and she'd heard what they were like. She needed to do something quick, and then along came a couple of spies – just what she wanted. Whoever said God moves in mysterious ways? There's nothing mysterious about God here. We find Rahab waiting for God, or at least God's spies. God was about to enter her life and turn it upside down – just as he does with ours, daily.

We see here several facets of God's care emerging from Rahab's intervention. Firstly a recognition of needs, secondly accepting responsibility to do something, thirdly deciding what she should do, and lastly taking a risk of being rejected when she offered them help – they could have said no and killed her.

How would we have responded in Rahab's place?

Prayer

Father, help me to discern where I should care. Help me to only offer the right care they need, not what I believe they would like. Help me to understand the person I'm caring for, accepting responsibility to care. Amen.

Memory verse

Psalm 18:30

As for God, his way is perfect; the word of the LORD is flawless. He is a shield for all who take refuge in him.

Action

Go and spend some time with someone who is not a Christian, just being with them, making friends.

Day 4

Being a caring Christian

A play in one act

Andrea (NVQ Angel) (Loud booming voice): And you are?

Christian (in a very refined voice): I'm 'The Bible Translator' and a Christian too, loved Jesus all my life I did, done everything the Bible said. So let me in and ... where's St Peter, isn't this his job?

Andrea (Louder voice): You want to complain eh, not good enough for you eh, want a different kind of heaven eh? Right you are. Peter, get yourself over here.

Peter (approaching Andrea with extreme caution): Ah Andrea, ermm, how you getting on? She's just started, transferred from packing wasn't it?

Andrea: Wants to complain this one.

Peter: Oh, just a sec then. Need to confirm the booking. Paul ... you there, definitely one for you.

Paul: Can't you deal with them yourself yet? Another eh?

Peter: Listen, mine's only a short book, few chapters. You wrote all that stuff about living. It's your problem.

Paul: Me? I was just on that road, going to, where was it? Some place called Damascus.

Peter: Yes, so you keep reminding us. Now go and get the other ledger will you.

Paul: No, ask James or someone. I've got practise to do.

Peter: Practise, practice, practice. All the time it's the practice. Not more still? Come on, you've had all this time. When's he coming back?

Paul: Who?

Peter: You know ... (nudging him), Jesus.

Paul: Jesus ... oh Jesus. I don't know, ask him yourself. But I'm still not getting the ledger.

Peter (calling out): James, James (looking around in vain), where is that boy? He's never around when you want him.

Paul: Tell me about it.

(James arrives)

Peter: James, run Christian75cvx1-34/1965 will you, HD version, and turn the sound down. You know my ears never really recovered from the last concert.

James: But the music's great at those Bible conventions, has to be loud.

Peter: Just run it, sound down.

(Sound of buttons being lightly pressed)

Peter: Skip that, and that, and that. Try around age 13ish, ermm, yes – there. What on earth's this?

Christian: Oh my teachers ... loved them all.

Peter: But you're screaming at them.

Peter: James, run it with subtitles will you? Oh ... can we edit that out ... ?

Paul: Jesus wants to see everything.

Peter: No, really? ... He wants everything?

Subtitles: I hate 'em, useless bunch, taught me nothing, hate all of 'em, just like primary school.

Peter: Now boyfriends, always helpful – boyfriends.

Subtitles: Boys, what do they know? You can't wear that, what will my friends think? No, I don't want more flowers. Mum, I am wearing that top and that skirt ... too short. Whatever.

Peter: Parents, always ... well really.

Subtitles: They died, then my brother to care for. I'm off. Just 'cause I'm the girl. No one's getting me to nurse him. There's homes ain't there.

Peter: Friends ...

Subtitles: Got rid of them. Always hanging around, wanting stuff.

Peter: A Missionary, you ... a missionary to real people ... live ones.

Subtitles: Finally, Bible translating, just me.

Peter: Ah, a wedding. I love weddings. All that cake, confetti, bells, more cake.

Subtitles: Marriage, mmmm, not those horrible girls, mummy this and mummy that, oh please.

Paul: Is there much more, I've filing to do?

James: 2 and a bit disks, plus commentary.

Peter: I'm beginning to see a pattern here. Could we jump to … bit further … the bit after … yes there – the plane crash. Play from here.

(Funeral, family supporting each other, deeply missed)

Paul (whispering to Peter): We got the right ending. They don't look upset or deeply missing, more like finally got rid of.

Christian: Well, honestly, just deeply missed. You wait till I see them. They'll know what missed is all about.

Peter: Look, can I just check, this is you we're watching?

Christian: Course it's me – you blind or something?

Paul: You did say you've done everything the Bible says? Bible, big book, with lots of little books? You sure you've come to the right place?

Christian: Nothing to do with me. I just arrived here. You think I'm not good enough to get in here do you? Listen, I know how this works. Isn't there some kind of appeal process? Who's in charge here? It's obviously not you lot, bickering all the time.

(Peter looks at Paul, who is busily looking in the other direction)

Peter and Paul together: Appeal process?

(Just then Jesus arrives)

Jesus: You two still arguing, and after all this time?

Jesus (to Christian): My child welcome. I love you and want you and need you. Welcome home.

Peter: Jesus, she did all those things ... upset all those people. What am I going to say to them if they come here?

Andrea: We could start another Missed Opportunity Support Group. The last one worked, well kind of. People did turn up, eventually.

Peter: OK, how about a Discover course. They're good, there's always lots of cake.

Paul: Discover courses? No not them – the other ones, the adventure things.

Andrea: Not those weekends away, bonding things. Yuck.

Jesus (ignoring the heated Andrea / Peter / Paul argument): Christian, it was your life, all of it, especially the hurtful bits. Come and see this. This is what I saw.

(Jesus and Christian sit and watch Christian's life DVD's)

Jesus: You see, nothing is ever wasted. See how you changed my world, my people. It's wonderful, thank you.

Peter [breaking off from Paul]: Jesus, where? When did she do any of that stuff? She didn't care about anyone, or what happened to any of them. She just ...

Jesus: There once was a man ...

Andrea & Peter & Paul: Quick hide, it's a parable.

Jesus: OK. No arguments. Paul, one of yours. How about your first letter to the Thessalonians, 5:12 to 22? Happy everyone?

(Nods all around)

Christian: When did I do any of those things? Look, to be honest, I'm not really a very nice person.

Jesus: You challenged my world. You made my people think about themselves. Then they could care for even more of my people, because of how you challenged them. Did I ever say the world worked in its own way? It's my way all the time. I turn the world upside down. It's an OK place anyway. Just wait till you see the next one. That will wow you! Anyway, I love you just as you are. I accept you as you are. I care for you just as you are. No matter what you've done, or where you've been, I love you.

Peter: Can I quote you on that one Jesus?

Jesus: Always.

Paul: OK, whose turn is it to make the tea? ... What? I'm trying to be more practical nowadays, more in touch with my inner apostle.

Epilogue

Each of us, despite the way we live, is still enfolded in Jesus love. Trying to understand why things happen, this side of heaven, usually proves a fruitless task. In speculation, we only see what is there. We fail to see the reasons for the being there, before our eyes.

Prayer

Father, I know you have a plan, especially for my life. Help me to build on what you have already started in me. Bring your plans to life through me. Amen.

Memory verse

Proverbs 2:6

For the Lord gives wisdom, and from his mouth come knowledge and understanding.

Action

Think of one person whom you have upset in the last week. Go and say, "I'm sorry, can I talk about it with you?"

Day 5

God so loved the world

Readings

Psalm 139:1-12

¹O LORD, you have searched me and you know me. ² You know when I sit and when I rise; you perceive my thoughts from afar. ³ You discern my going out and my lying down; you are familiar with all my ways. ⁴ Before a word is on my tongue you know it completely, O LORD. ⁵ You hem me in—behind and before; you have laid your hand upon me. ⁶ Such knowledge is too wonderful for me, too lofty for me to attain. ⁷ Where can I go from your Spirit? Where can I flee from your presence? ⁸ If I go up to the heavens, you are there; if I make my bed in the depths, you are there. ⁹ If I rise on the wings of the dawn, if I settle on the far side of the sea, ¹⁰ even there your hand will guide me, your right hand will hold me fast. ¹¹ If I say, "Surely the darkness will hide me and the light become night around me," ¹² even the darkness will not be dark to you; the night will shine like the day, for darkness is as light to you.

Romans 8:38-40

³⁸ For I am convinced that neither death nor life, neither angels nor demons, neither the present nor the future, nor any powers, ³⁹ neither height nor depth, nor anything else in all creation, will be able to separate us from the love of God that is in Christ Jesus our Lord.

John 3:16

[16] "For God so loved the world that he gave his one and only Son, that whoever believes in him shall not perish but have eternal life.

Meditation

When all seems endless and sad, when there seems to be nothing left to say to make amends, when there is only darkness and pain, there is Jesus saying, "Come to Me, I care."

Over the years I have attended a few funerals, those of my parents, relatives, and on one occasion a friend a little older than me. On this occasion, as we entered the church it was as if all the love had been sucked out. When the minister entered he was reading the passage above, quite quietly, almost stumbling over some of the words. Behind him came my friend's coffin, with those words marching around the packed church, daring anyone to contradict them, saying, "One day that will be you." One day someone will walk before your coffin reading these words and you will be silent, unlistening, inside your coffin where you will no longer hear them.

John 3:16 is an oft quoted passage at funerals. It comes from the beginning of a discourse on Jesus' life: one of sadness and joy. Sadness, for men reject Jesus God's promised Son, the Light [which] has come into the world. They love darkness instead of light, because their deeds are evil (John 3:19). Joy, because only through Him is there hope for our world. He who lives by the truth comes into the light (John 3:21). Paul, in AD 50, speaks of this light as he writes to the church in Thessalonica: "You are all sons of the light and sons of the day. We do not belong to the night or the darkness. So then, let us not be like others, who are asleep, but let us be alert and self controlled" (1Thessalonians 5:5,6).

And what of this darkness, the sadness funerals bring? Where is the light in all this sadness? This is the Light that is constant when the world seems full of funerals. When all the tears are cried for painful loss, there is Jesus saying, "Come to me, I'm crying too. Come and share your sadness with me. I care." Only the devil stands in the way of this care, delighting in our darkness, laughing at those who tread his paths. He laughs as they deceive themselves into believing they're OK. The devil knows they're not, which is why he laughs so much. He does not care. Indeed, he seeks to steal from us what care there is.

Jesus knew this darkness too, as John reminds us: "The Light shines in the darkness, and the darkness has not understood it" (John 1:5). Darkness will never understand, because of what it represents: a void without the love to care. The world cares not, peddling darkness and despair to all; but we may choose a different path, and it is our choice, as no one asks us to care about our world. We can just walk away and no one minds. It's acceptable, the right thing to do. Why should we get involved when we don't know them? They're so far away in another country it doesn't really matter. Someone else will care, won't they? And still there's more need, more care than I can give. So why should I care? I've problems of my own. No one cares for me.

If I go to the farthest field, or hide in the deepest cave, so far away that there can never be anyone else there, there is Jesus waiting for me, ready to share my grief, my pain and sadness, no matter what I've done or how I've got there.

I'm not good at funerals – too much coffin and flowers. It all looks too real to be true. It can't really have happened, not to them; but it has, and now we're at that point of saying goodbye. And the coffin is slowly going, and then they're gone, and we're left standing, alone. Loss is a reality. The pain goes away eventually, well most of it. The rest we can try and hide, or hide from it. All the Gospels portray images of uncontrollable despair at Jesus' cross. This could not be happening, not this, no. How? Not to Him. Without the loss, the sacrifice, there is no gain, no heaven, just a painful earth.

There is no care unless we make a sacrifice, even a tiny one. Will we take a moment's thought, or pause in the chat or the busyness of our day, to come outside ourselves and stand in the shoes of the person who owns no shoes, who craves not the leftovers from our meal but the food we've thrown in the bin?

Do I care? Can I care for him? Someone should, but why me? Surely there's someone else – there always is. Sometimes there isn't. It's just us, no one else. And I'm no good at caring. I don't know what to say or do, how to start or finish a conversation. Sometimes at funerals, care is saying hello and listening. At other times our care may need to be a little more proactive. There is always someone with a need, wanting our time, and expecting us to drop everything and be with them, just because they have a need or want someone to talk to. In all of this Jesus is asking a question: whether we care just enough to go and say, "How are you?" Most of us can say a little, or nothing. Just being there is often words enough.

At Jesus' funeral there weren't many people to listen to – not many turned up: Joseph, Nicodemus, and two women – Mary Magdalene and the other Mary. The guards arrived a little later to make sure no one wandered off with any dead bodies.

God Himself knows loss, and He knows how loss affects us. He fully understands the painful experience of loss, the sadness of utter defeat. He heard the devil laughing as His plans for mankind seemingly went wrong. Jesus, like all men, was destined to die. God lost His own Son on a cross for us, dying so we might have life.

If you attend a Good Friday service, you will find that readers often pause following the words, "And Jesus died ..."

The real event was quite a busy affair if you read the accounts: noisy, sweaty, full of emotion. There was no quiet pause for the Son of Man as He gave us life eternal. But in the Easter services there is a pause. A pause occurs too in the funeral service, at the act of committal. This is a pause to think. Could we have done more, said more, loved more, or cared more? We can do no more for the deceased. They're gone now. But we can care for the living. Take a look around you, at the next funeral service you attend. Who could do with a little help and care right now?

Prayer

Father, show me more of your love and your presence in our world. Help me to see you in everything around me. Thank you for the love you bring into my life and the care you show to me. Grant me opportunities to share this same love and care that you have shown to me, to others around me. Amen.

Memory verse

John 11:25-26

[25] ..."I am the resurrection and the life. He who believes in me will live, even though he dies; [26] and whoever lives and believes in me will never die..."

Action

Is there someone who has annoyed or upset you recently? See if they would mind if you asked them for a chat about how they are, or about their day, or prayed with them a short prayer, if appropriate. If not, is there someone you have upset? Ask them how they are? Maybe seek them out for a chat, or a prayer.

Day 6

God caring

Reading: Revelation 21:1-5

A New Heaven and a New Earth

¹Then I saw a new heaven and a new earth, for the first heaven and the first earth had passed away, and there was no longer any sea. ² I saw the Holy City, the new Jerusalem, coming down out of heaven from God, prepared as a bride beautifully dressed for her husband. ³ And I heard a loud voice from the throne saying, "Now the dwelling of God is with men, and he will live with them. They will be his people, and God himself will be with them and be their God. ⁴ He will wipe every tear from their eyes. There will be no more death or mourning or crying or pain, for the old order of things has passed away." ⁵ He who was seated on the throne said, "I am making everything new!" Then he said, "Write this down, for these words are trustworthy and true."

Meditation

What a mess the world is in. What's happened to it? Look at the state the planet's in. It started out so well, only to find itself trashed in a matter of weeks. And that was only the beginning of God's plan. Look at the other end – Revelation. What's all that about, with its strange allusions to new beginnings? It's a wonder it became the closing book of the New Testament. And then we have the bit in the middle. We're told we should be looking out for each other's needs, as the earth travels through time.

Amongst all that's goings on around us, the busyness of life, the 'keeping ourselves going', there's God with one of His purposes. King David endured them, Moses, I'm sure, got fed up with them, and Paul was good at quoting them. It usually takes a little while to unpack a purpose and work out what He wants. This time God wants us, the incredibly busy ones, our lives already jammed with good intentions, to add another one: to use our time and our resources to care as He would care. Such is God and His purposes.

Each and every day, God manifests His purpose of caring, which is to care through us. He cares for us, so we can care for those around us. And here's the sticky bit: I'm not very good at caring for others. I have enough to cope with just looking after me.

So how did Revelation make it as the final book? There's certainly nothing concluding about it. It points quite categorically into the future. It also points to us as part of that future, changed to be as we should have been, as we were before the fall, before it all went pear shaped. Revelation presents unremitting evidence of how God will finally conclude this earth and make a fresh one, glittering in the new dawning sunlight.

For many, journeying there is pain and sadness, a route also trodden by God. Joy breaks into tears and tears merge into happiness, a pattern repetitious in its daily stride. God promises that one day we'll really arrive there, where there's no more sadness, pain, or tears, and a stupendous moment of 'Revelation'. The old earth with its heaven is overwhelmed, and replaced by one all shiny and new, as it should have been (at least till we started doing the sin thing – not our fault, we just got lead astray, didn't we? Well, almost!)

Our relationship with God too will change. No longer will there be a separation. God will be physically present again, walking and talking with us, united with us in a way only glimpsed at in Genesis. We will have His whole self all to ourselves, for the whole eternity. How we relate to him will change too: "And I heard a loud voice from the throne saying 'Now the dwelling of

God is with men, and he will live with them. They will be his people, and God himself will be with them and be their God'" (Revelation 21:3).

God will be with us, a kind of Christmas day every day: "… He will live with them" (καὶ σκηνώσει μετ' αὐτῶν). The original Greek is quite forceful. It's more, "and he will 'abide / fix' 'a tabernacle / to dwell' in with them." The word 'live' is a little tame. God has not just shifted Himself. He's moved His whole operation, His tabernacle. That's how much He cares. No longer wanting to be in heaven, He's packed His bags and gone to where His people are. He has 'sent' Himself. Not just Jesus and the Holy Spirit. This time we get the whole Trinity.

As God prepares to send himself, He asks us to prepare to go too. Next door, next country, next continent, who knows? (Well God does of course). If God cares enough to send Himself, He certainly cares enough to send us, His children, to where we need to be.

Sending is twofold: us, or something we have. That something is usually money. If I can't go, I can give some money so you can go instead. It works very well. We might be more useful to God by our giving than by our going. Each year many churches run Gift Days with lots of preparative 'giving' talks. I'm considerably challenged by the talks on 'not giving' and what will happen. Money's a funny thing. Our world encroaches on our finances, pressurising us to buy what we can't afford, putting desires in my heart for that little gift to me. Do these solve my latest crush on worldly pleasures – the new smart phone, new bed, new …? Do I need it? Yes, of course I need it. I can justify it so well to myself. I always do, because I 'need it', I don't just 'want' it? That's me. What about the rest of the world?

A saddening event in recent times is third world farmers abandoning whole crops of coco beans, as the beans would fetch so little. It's too expensive even to pick them. Maybe we could help: move there and start picking his beans for free; pay someone to pick them for us; change our coffee buying habits so that growers get a fair deal for their beans. His beans are beans of sadness. They need picking to relieve his pain.

Revelation points to a time in the future when, "there will be no more death or mourning or crying or pain, for the old order of things has passed away" (Revelation 21:5). Why wait? Why can't we have it now? I hate waiting. Christmas day everyday would be amazing. With Jesus, the order changed. Sin was vanquished from our planet, but it still skulks around trying for a comeback, infecting lives to destruction, pretending nothing's changed. We may not have the new planet yet, but there's no reason why we can't live in the new world, the Revelation 21:5 world. The planet will just have to catch us up later.

I'm not sure if we grow coco beans in the UK. What is around us are multitudes of other beans ready for picking, but we need to let God show us where they are. Where are the needs of our neighbours – the beans of sorrow and tears, the beans of hate and destruction, the beans of loneliness and pain? If we pick them, we can take them out of our neighbour's life, showing that we care. In their place we may give fruits of hope, joy, and love, just as God gave to each of us, pressed down and overflowing.

As our world waits to one day stop its spinning course through time, so God waits too. The interim is filled with a question that God will one day ask us all, "So tell me: what did you do with your time on earth? How many coco beans did you pick?" It's sometimes hard to find the beans. Sometimes a person buries them so far down they are almost invisible. We don't know where to start in helping them. Other times they lie on the ground around us, or on shelves in shops and supermarkets, waiting for collection. Do we pick them up, or do we pay someone else to collect them for us? God is happy with either choice, but we should do one or the other, because one day He's going to ask about the beans.

Prayer

Father, help me to see your need in my world around me. Help me to see where you would have me serve you, in whatever capacity you would have me be. Amen

Memory verses

Psalm 113:7-8

[7] He raises the poor from the dust and lifts the needy from the ash heap; [8] he seats them with princes, with the princes of their people.

Action

Tea or coffee is nice to drink. If it's fairly traded it often helps the growers just to make ends meet. Today, as on other days, you may need a 'pick you up'. Have some tea or coffee today with someone you don't know too well. Do they have some beans which need picking, or perhaps do you?

Day 7

Being alive to God and caring

Reading: John 15:1-15

The Vine and the Branches

¹ "I am the true vine, and my Father is the gardener. ² He cuts off every branch in me that bears no fruit, while every branch that does bear fruit he prunes so that it will be even more fruitful. ³ You are already clean because of the word I have spoken to you. ⁴ Remain in me, and I will remain in you. No branch can bear fruit by itself; it must remain in the vine. Neither can you bear fruit unless you remain in me.

⁵ "I am the vine; you are the branches. If a man remains in me and I in him, he will bear much fruit; apart from me you can do nothing. ⁶ If anyone does not remain in me, he is like a branch that is thrown away and withers; such branches are picked up, thrown into the fire and burned. ⁷ If you remain in me and my words remain in you, ask whatever you wish, and it will be given you. ⁸ This is to my Father's glory, that you bear much fruit, showing yourselves to be my disciples.

⁹ "As the Father has loved me, so have I loved you. Now remain in my love. ¹⁰ If you obey my commands, you will remain in my love, just as I have obeyed my Father's commands and remain in his love. ¹¹ I have told you this so that my joy may be in you and that your joy may be complete. ¹² My command is this: Love each other as I have loved you. ¹³ Greater love has no one than this, that he lay down his life for his friends. ¹⁴ You are my friends if you do what I command. ¹⁵ I no longer call you servants, because a servant does not know his master's business. Instead, I have called you friends, for everything that I learned from my Father I have made known to you.

Meditation

Have you ever found some forgotten piece of clothing hiding behind your wardrobe, or tidied out your shed and found those lingering seed packets? Fashions change, and seeds no longer take root. They reach a point where they're no good to anyone anymore. God finds things lurking, things almost forgotten that are no longer useful and that no longer bear fruit. God is a ruthless gardener. If it does not work, out it goes. No fruit – no existence. At the same time, He carefully prunes those shoots that show promise, the ones serving His purpose. Why such ruthlessness? Because retaining plants that grow in the wrong direction, plants that are flowerless or fruitless, or plants that are plainly diseased, causes more damage to arise. Cutting is severe, but sometimes it is the only way.

Lying in bed, we can decide whether to get up or not, or whether to have tea or coffee this morning. But is it our choice, or another's influence? Choices can take us away from friends and family. They can break the hoped for dreams of others. Pursuing our ambitions we may rush hastily into crisis, achieving success at the expense of others, reaching a point where it's us and them, separate. Until, perhaps, we remember and reflect: "I'm sorry. I think I know who you're talking about …" Like us God the pruner also feels pain on separation, a pain there should never have been. Because He cares what happens to His children, He cuts from our lives the destructive parts, those things that lead us away from the life He knows we can have. True gardeners spend hours cutting tiny lifeless bits from plants. Only as a last resort do they dig up the entire plant and throw it away. God is the same. Cutting someone completely off is His last resort.

They may have made their choices as to who they follow, rejecting God, but He still loves them, albeit not their thoughts or actions. Just as there is great rejoicing over one sinner who repents, there is great sadness over one who turns his back on God.

Pruning is no fun either, but there isn't another way for us to become what God would have us to be. With gentle pruning a plant will push up more hardy, more resilient than before, more able to stand and resist. If we refrain from pruning, firstly we show how little we care for the welfare of our plants; secondly, the plant grows unchallenged and undirected; thirdly, we abdicate our care and the plans we have for the plant's future.

However, there's a 'but'! Unlike a plant bought from the garden store, we have a choice of coming and settling into God's garden. This is where other Christians are important. Jesus' great commission is to, "Go and make disciples of all the world." Plants or people will not be able to come into God's garden unless we His followers invite them in. We can choose to show them the love and care that we have already received from Him, and the love and care that they would receive from the pruning hand of God in their lives. How do plants make it into God's garden? From us, who are already members of the garden, sharing what we have found with God as our gardener.

Getting plants into God's garden is no easy task. Once they're there they can see the benefits. However, as an outsider looking into the garden, into our churches, what do they see? Do they see Spring and Summer, or a 'Winter of discontent'? Whatever they see, so too does the Gardener. And gardeners eventually come with shears, for pruning or cutting.

God shows His pruning in the incidents and developments of life. He prunes in a moment, having chosen from amongst the subtle shades of good and evil existent in our lives. His every intervention is characterised by His love: sowing, watering, nurturing, feeding, moving, weeding, pruning, and cutting. God goes to all this trouble, not because He needs us, but because He loves us. He asks of those who submit to His pruning to "…love each other as I have loved you" (John15:12). It is as we remain loved by God as our gardener that we are able to love and care for others.

What of the care shown by those not attached to God's vine? God our gardener directs how His children act, calling all to come in and share His garden. The act of coming into the garden and our life in the garden are private and unseen. God works subtly in every area of our life. God sees the interior of a life, but we just see the outside person. We cannot perceive where a person is in their journey with God. At the same time, living in God's world, created by Him and populated by Him, it would be impossible to find a place where God is not. God the gardener's influence seeps into the world, manifesting itself outside the garden, in all the world around us.

And to us, as members of God's garden, is tasked a challenge: to love and care for God's world, even the world outside His garden. We see this in the ordinariness of Christian life around us. It is almost impossible to be a Christian and not to care. Our care is shown in how we react to needs, how we feel that we should be doing something, how we think about our friends and relatives. There's no getting away from God, unless you step off the planet. Even then, it's reported how beautiful the planet looks from space. God seems to be everywhere, even in space.

How can we stick close to the Gardener and the caring work He asks of us? Through seeking out the Gardener daily. Gardens and plants are daily adventures. If you forget about them for a day, all sorts of things happen. God talks about us remaining in Him, which is how any plant/gardener relationship works best. Plants rarely get up and walk off, but that's a choice we have as Christians. We can choose to remain, or move out. If we leave, we would miss out on the care offered by God our gardener. John says, "… Instead, I have called you friends, for everything that I learned from my Father I have made known to you" (John 15:15). Jesus invites us to stay, not as servants, but as friends, to share His Fathers joys, comforts, and care. We grow through our friendship with God the gardener.

And what of those who are cut off? People don't have to follow God, they can always leave. We don't have to accept His care. There is always another option, as John 15 describes. We who remain in the garden have a responsibility of showing God's love and care to the world, even to those cut off from God. It is never too late to change your mind and come back into the garden. As gardeners know, if you cut off a shoot and plant it afresh in good and nurturing soil, it comes up as vigorous as ever, ready to be a useful plant in your garden. All it takes from us is to go and find the lost cuttings, so they too may return to God's garden.

Prayer

Father, send me into your garden to collect both seeds and plants. Help me to be your sower, scattering seeds and nurturing people in their journey or their discovery of you. Help me to see you in those around me, their needs and desires. Let me be the one to meet them and direct them towards you. Amen

Memory verse

Proverbs 23:12

Apply your heart to instruction and your ears to words of knowledge.

Action

Today is all about being in the garden, although at the moment it's still a bit wet, and some places have snow. Find someone you know who's been having a rough time, buy them some flowers or just one, and go and see how they're getting on.

Day 8

Love one another

Reading: 1 John 4:11

[11] Dear friends, since God so loved us, we also ought to love one another.

Meditation

Do you realise that it takes three to love: the person doing the loving, the one receiving the love, and the person (Jesus) effecting the change to love in the first place?

Do we love one another? Evidence suggests not always. Brothers and sisters fight; relatives argue and seek legal advice; friends stop speaking to each other. Few situations change; even Jesus' own disciples argued. Despite being social creatures, surprisingly we don't get on, not really. There's tolerance, acceptance and understanding, but often no real getting on. We'll have to wait till we get to heaven to properly get on with each other.

In the interim we find God hard at work sorting out His wayward children.

Take for instance God's chosen people, the Jewish nation. Nations often arise from local tribal squabbles, and the ascent of Israel was no different, complete with internal feuds and brutal battles. Later the itinerant desert Israelites even criticised Moses' poor catering facilities, making endless complaints about water shortages (Exodus 17) and refusing to agree with him when he was asked to mediate for them.

Where fights did break out the rules were quite prescriptive. If two men are fighting and the wife of one of them comes to rescue her husband from his assailant, and she reaches out and seizes him by his genitals, you shall cut off her hand. Show her no pity (Deuteronomy 25:10-12). Married women beware!

Resolving territorial disputes seems no better, actually quite gory. In 2 Samuel 2:13-16 we find Abner (Saul's Commander) and Joab (David's Commander) arriving at the pool of Gibeon. Each chooses twelve young men, who then grab their opponents head and thrust their daggers into each other and fight. OK, could be worse! We may find it hard to conceive such brutality associated with God's nation.

The New Testament also relates conflict, but with not so much actual damage. We see disagreements amongst Jesus' own disciples as to who's the greatest. The disciples argued all the way to Capernaum over this. Arriving there and realising Jesus had been listening all the time produced some very quiet disciples. Jesus says to them, "If anyone wants to be first, he must be the very last and the servant of all" (Mark 9:35). Taking a little child in his arms, Jesus says, "Whoever welcomes one of these little children in my name welcomes me; and whoever welcomes me does not welcome me but the one who sent me" (Mark 9:37).

Likewise, in Acts chapter 15 we find Paul and Barnabas in the Antioch of AD 50, arguing. After an unfortunate 'sharp disagreement' on evangelistic arrangements, Paul (accompanied by Silas) heads off to Tarsus, whilst Barnabas (accompanied by Mark) goes over to Cyprus. What was the reason for splitting? Their disagreement was partly over Mark, but also over allegiances. Here Luke uses the word παροξυσμός, often translated as sharp disagreement or irritation. Irritation is perhaps more Luke the medics term. This irritation stems from previous allegiances made by Barnabas favouring Jewish-Christians (Galatians 2:13). Meanwhile, Paul's mind is beginning to focus on the Gentile world.

The love God has for us needs to be demonstrated to the world, not squandered in bickering disputes. Consider God as the third person in these arguments. Paul and Barnabas disagreed, but out from this flows Gods love for Jews and Gentiles alike, as God intervenes. Barnabas takes charge of

Mark's life, with Mark growing into someone that Paul in later life wants as his companion. Strange though it might seem, by arguing we allow ourselves to become better known by another, often turning enemies into friends under God's influence.

How can I love someone, even the irritating ones? We can't, as all we see is the irritating unpleasantness they portray. To see what they could become with our love and care, we need Jesus to change how we see them, seeing them though His eyes, not ours.

To change our view requires we start by caring for ourselves and accepting the love Jesus offers. Jesus shows how, without His love in our lives, we remain trapped forever inside our own perceptions of what love is. Jesus has to love us and teach us how to care, before we can hope to love another. We need God's healing to love, just as King David, Moses, Abraham, and countless others did. They first submitted to God's love for them, before they could truly love another. And that's the hard bit – letting another know us enough to love us. It's so easy to do something for someone else. It's much harder to let someone do something for us. We prefer others to see our strong and self reliant selves. Not the one hiding in the corner crying with pain and doubt about how the world's been treating us.

Young children crave attention: the 'always me'. Adults too crave attention, the always me, except it often becomes the selfish me. Into this embittered selfish world Jesus sends us, asking us to go and make a difference. But I'm hopeless at making differences. I'm off to Tarshish (Jonah 1:3) – much safer. Jonah found, and we must too, that there are parts of our lives not yet inhabited by God, parts we've tried to keep from Him, hoping He'd never notice. God craves to love us, all of us, not just the bits we want Him to love. It's only because God loved us first, that we can ever hope to love one another.

All it takes is a single act to love another, which for many of us is extremely hard to do: "I don't like that person," "I have enough of my own issues before I consider theirs too," "I'm having money problems," "After I've said hello what then?"

Start small – a smile, a handshake, a cup of tea or coffee, a hug, a listening ear, some food, another smile maybe tomorrow, a "Hello, how are you?" – to the person who one day grows up and changes the world as we never could, all because we first smiled.

Worth a try?

Prayer

Father, help me to see where wounds need healing both in my life and in the lives of those around me. Give the courage to say sorry and make amends to those I have injured or hurt. Help me see how to restore the love you have for them, building a relationship with them, built on your love and care.

Memory verse

James 1:22

Do not merely listen to the word, and so deceive yourselves. Do what it says.

Action

Who do you know who does not like you too well? It could be someone you had a row with ages ago, or yesterday. Or it could be someone who you thought was a friend and has let you down badly. It is to these people we need to share the love we have received from God. As he forgives us, so too should we forgive others, asking in return for their forgiveness. Do we know of anyone falling into these categories? See how far you can go in making contact and trying to retrieve what has been lost, seeking forgiveness where needed.

Day 9

Caring for ourselves

Readings

Proverbs 28:26

²⁶ He who trusts in himself is a fool, but he who walks in wisdom is kept safe.

Matthew 7:24-27

The Wise and Foolish Builders

²⁴ "Therefore everyone who hears these words of mine and puts them into practice is like a wise man who built his house on the rock. ²⁵ The rain came down, the streams rose, and the winds blew and beat against that house; yet it did not fall, because it had its foundation on the rock. ²⁶ But everyone who hears these words of mine and does not put them into practice is like a foolish man who built his house on sand. ²⁷ The rain came down, the streams rose, and the winds blew and beat against that house, and it fell with a great crash."

Meditation

How well do we know ourselves, our likes and dislikes, how we make decisions, what motivates us, what we build our lives on? Mostly pretty well, but what if we're challenged on something we're not sure of? How do we decide then? Some choose to ignore decisions, others rush in quickly with an idea, some linger on the side dithering around, and others stay where they are, not changing at all. There's nothing wrong with these, provided we've spent some time thinking before we jump in.

Decision making is tied up with where we place our trust; in us, in other people, in God; and we get to choose. If it's only ever me involved in deciding, I'm looking for an answer alone, with my thoughts and experiences circling around. As soon as I ask someone else, I gain their entire life's experiences. I may disagree with what they say, but it's not only me, I've found a friend to ask. We are social creatures, because that's how God designed us. He didn't design us to exist in isolation. If we're looking for someone with an awful lot of life experiences, we can always ask God what He thinks (and we still get to disagree). God hopes we will ask Him, sharing with Him as a friend we can rely on when things don't go our way, someone we can trust with our lives. It's like building a house.

Building of any description (lives included) requires insight into what will work and how to achieve it, essentially a plan. Just like house builders, we need to know what the end result will look like and what we need to get there. House builders (in any age) require some basic knowledge of surveying and construction techniques. If we're asked to build a shed from scratch, we would prepare for it; in building our lives, it's not always so. We often take life as it comes, waiting to see what happens next, occasionally with a little light planning. Thankfully builders are not like this, recklessly putting up structures believing they'll stand, with no regard for building regulations; unlike one of the builders we meet in Jesus' story.

Jesus, being a practical man, knows the Palestinian landscape: dried summer valleys, awash with winter torrents sweeping away all in their path. And here we find our two builders with an idea – let's build a house. Both actually do build their houses. It's the foundations which are the issue. So why does one choose rock and the other sand? It's all about listening and doing.

Notice that both houses stand until the storms come. Without it being bashed about neither builder would have know how well his house was built.

The sand builder relied on his own abilities of building, thinking it was fine, when in reality there was a huge problem he couldn't see – his foundations didn't exist. Imagine buying a house, your dream home. The survey's done and shows the house is good, but it lacks foundations. It's been standing for a while, so may survive a storm. Do you still buy it? Hopefully not! But what if you're already sitting in the house without foundations, and the storm is on its way, what then?

Trusting in ourselves presupposes we're extremely good at life management. We don't need any assistance as we can do it alone. If we only ever trust ourselves, we may grow a bit, but not reach our completeness. We may look good on the outside, but have disastrous foundations inside. We need someone we trust to say the hard things to us like, "Why on earth have you built it here? What's wrong with the rocks?" The builders had a choice of where to build. Jesus presents us with a choice: listen to what He says and use that as a basis for life, or not – our choice.

And what if Jesus never came? Would it have made any difference to how we live? We know from non Biblical records that someone called Jesus lived in Palestine, causing problems and challenging authority, and was crucified around AD30. If no Jesus, why bother to care about anyone ourselves? We can never get it right. Jesus shows how lives can be built on something which works and makes us strong. Alternatively, you can always choose to build on the sand. Just don't be there when the storm hits.

House building and life building are both practical activities, and that's the point. We must be people who put into practice what Jesus says. No sitting around thinking and talking about it. In order to obey Jesus, we must understand ourselves, seeing what needs changing. Jesus here teaches a practical lesson (otherwise why use builders?): are we wise or foolish in what we do, what we put into practice? If we are feeling like a foolish builder, what's brought us to this place, and what's stopping us changing? It's often our own thoughts: how helpless we feel to change or to make a difference. It may all seem too much for us, so we learned how to be helpless or hopeless.

If we spend our lives thinking we've built on the sand and that's the end of it, we will never change. It's a question of what we spend our time thinking about. If we're optimistic and resilient we can move rocky mountains, but if our thoughts centre around "I can't do that" hope and resilience wane and we become a bit of a foolish builder. We've all been there, and periodically will return there, which oddly is not always a bad place to be! A house falling flat will soon make us reconsider our life's direction and who's in control, who we're obeying. Likewise, unless we get it wrong, we never grow. Trying to get perfection first time out doesn't work. We need the practice. Knowing what it's like to get it wrong or to face obstacles helps us grow. In our failures we develop resilience, becoming more able to overcome the difficulty next time.

Jesus is a practical teacher and knows what we're like. He knows how we'll be tempted and what will help us grow. The passage of the wise and foolish builders comes at the end of three chapters on Jesus' teachings about life and living. He's asking us to consider the practicalities of how we live our lives. If our foundations are not on Him, we may build a very fine house which to the world looks quite impressive, but when life gets a bit rough, will what we've built stand?

We can choose in whose wisdom we walk: in ours alone trying to work out life, in that of our friends with their own experiences, or with God. We still get to make decisions about how we live. Even if it turns out a bit foolish, next time we know we'll be better. God understands all about foolish builders as He made them too.

Prayer

Father, I realise that my life can only be built on you. Help me to see where you are, so I can build and centre my life around you. Help me to share what I have found with other builders, both in my community and in my church.

Where my building needs redirection, gently help me to reconstruct my life, building in the direction you would have me go. Amen

Memory verse

2 Corinthians 5:17

Therefore, if anyone is in Christ, he is a new creation; the old has gone, the new has come!

Action

Sit and write a list of all the ways you could help your community with your gifts, talents, specials skills or abilities. Pray over your list, asking God to show you where He could use your own special talents for the service of others. Then go and have a chat to your church leaders about where you could serve more in your church or community.

Day 10

Trusting in God - faith and mountains

Readings

Matthew 17:20

[20]... I tell you the truth, if you have faith as small as a mustard seed, you can say to this mountain, 'Move from here to there' and it will move. Nothing will be impossible for you.

Mark 11:23

[23]... if anyone says to this mountain, 'Go, throw yourself into the sea,' and does not doubt in his heart but believes that what he says will happen, it will be done for him.

1 Corinthians 13:2

[2]... if I have a faith that can move mountains, but have not love, I am nothing.

Meditation

What is it with mountains? The ones in the Blue Mountain range near Katomba Australia are quite blue in the early mornings, but it's their enormity which gets you. The Bible too speaks of mountains: we have Moses clambering up and down them, Nebuchadnezzar having nightmares about them, and Jesus speaks of hurling them into the sea (something for the next Olympics?). Mountains, it seems, represent the impossible movable object. However, with a sufficiency of faith the mountain moves (cartographers beware).

Jesus teaches about portable mountains, not to upset the geo-physics community, or to finally thwart the Pharisees, but because mountains really do move ever so gently. Moving is part of being a mountain. They're not static objects. They shift, ever so slightly, even when there's no throwing intended.

In our journey through life, we affect the lives of people we meet, often ever so slightly. Just as mountains gently move, what we say and do affects others, sometimes ever so slightly. It might not be as noticeable as the Blue Mountains splashing into the South Pacific ocean but our words and actions are making a difference.

Our response to God's influence shifts the world ever so slightly. We're already mountain movers, we just haven't realised it yet. They move not necessarily because we say so, but stemming from our love. Jesus tells His disciples, "… if I have a faith that can move mountains, but have not love, I am nothing" (1 Corinthians 13:2). Love is an essential ingredient to the mountain moving. If the mountain picks its skirts up and steps aside without love, why bother asking it to move in the first place?

Mountains, as we know from our own clamberings, differ in size, shape, texture, views, snow or rock face. Tackling such mountain moving requires faith to believe they'll move. Mountain moving faith stems from belief, trust, God's word (the Bible), our relationship with Him, and prayer; these unite, driving our faith. With these united, the enormous impossibility of mountain removal (rampant with climbers and map makers in case of imminent disappearance) becomes reality.

- Belief – seeing how we can change lives
- Trust – in what we are doing – it's what God wants us to be about
- The Bible – seeing its relevance to everything in our lives

- Relationship – with God as Father, Creator, and Instigator
- Prayer – responding to and seeking guidance from God

Why then are we disappointed when prayers seemingly go unanswered and the mountain is not hurled into the ocean? We may crave to see mountain hurling, but what we get is little shudders. Does God care that my mountain's not in the sea? Jesus said of faith, "Whatever you ask in prayer, you will receive it, if you have faith" (Matthew 21:22). But we didn't get the mountain splash so God didn't answer, God doesn't care anymore. We should consider here how and why mountains are moved in the first place.

It is outside God's nature not to care for us. So we need to see how God intervenes. Our expectations are often mountain moving whereas God's are frequently much smaller. What are we looking for? What is God looking for? And what's the difference between them? Usually its small hills though could be bumps in the road, or equally mountains; but there is a difference.

God's ultimate care is one of drawing us to Himself. He wants the very best for us. We currently live in a fallen world, subject to the devil's whims. God knows this, as well as the pain our lives may be full of. God also knows that, at some point in the future, He'll destroy this world, making another, a better one. It is to this new world that He calls all who believe in Him. Jesus, in comforting His disciples, said that He was going to prepare a place for us (John 14:2), and God is making a new world just for us. God does care about what's going on.

Prayers are answered and people are healed, often for a purpose, God's purpose. For example, Jesus heals Peter's mother in law (Mark 1:30-31) who then sorts out the catering, with the help of the disciples I'm sure. We all need caring for, and God will find the right person for the job.

In asking God to intervene, we ask Him to provide the best for our friends, relatives, and neighbours. We often have mountainous ideas which may be different from the ones which are best for them, the ones God knows all about. We believe this person will be healed – some are, some are not; it tests our reliance on God no end.

It's not that we lack faith to move mountains. It's just that the mountains look different from where God is standing.

There is another side to faith: the 'strength in adversity, standing up to the trials of this world kind of faith', as Paul experienced in Rome. We find him once again imprisoned by Nero (this time not under house arrest, but in a cold cell). He's writing to Timothy, encouraging him to be strong and faithful, for God is with us (2 Timothy 1). Paul would have loved to have been released from there, allowing him to continue his missionary work. Eventually he's killed, but not before he's spent all his last efforts writing. If Paul had been on the road evangelising, he might not have had the time to write all his letters, which form a large chunk of our Bible. God had a purpose in keeping Paul locked up, so he could write for us. God cared so much for Paul that he wanted him to be spared the rigours of travel. As it is, his writings perhaps reached more people than Paul himself could ever have done.

Lastly, our response to faith: as we have faith in God, God is faithful to us. Once our mountain's shuffled out, or maybe wobbled around, we come closer to God. Through this experience we see how God does move mountains, usually the small and daily versions, but bigger ones too. We see how approachable He is, how He responds to our needs – the care we want to give, the hurting pain we wish removed. Jesus reminds us to ask. How much asking do we do, a little or a lot? If we don't ask, then the mountain's going to stay put.

"Ask and it will be given to you, pressed down and overflowing".

Jesus Christ, Son of God

Prayer

Father, help me in the timidity of my prayers to trust you to move more mountains of my life? Show me where you are already working in my life and the mountains you have moved for me. Lord, I pray to receive more of your love and care, and more mountain shifting in my life. Help me Lord to share the wondrous love you give to me, with others around me, as we challenge the mountains in our lives to be thrown into the sea. Amen.

Memory verse

Matthew 7:7

Ask and it will be given to you; seek and you will find; knock and the door will be opened to you.

Action

At the end of a busy week, spend some time with a friend, a loved one, a brother or sister, or your next door neighbour, telling them how your week's been and what you liked and disliked about it. Ask them how theirs has been and how they think they could improve next week. Perhaps next week might be better with more God in it. If it seems appropriate, pray with them about the coming week, or pray later about the things you have discussed with them.

Day 11

How to ignore the world and get away with it

Reading: Matthew 25:37-40

[37]... 'Lord, when did we see you hungry and feed you, or thirsty and give you something to drink? [38] When did we see you a stranger and invite you in, or needing clothes and clothe you? [39] When did we see you sick or in prison and go to visit you?' [40] The King will reply, 'I tell you the truth, whatever you did for one of the least of these brothers of mine, you did for me.'

Meditation

Around me is the maddening crowd; inside me perhaps is just madness, how do I tell?

Madness here is not a suffering illness where skilled care and comfort is needed; this is more our daily struggles of life as Christians in a world of maddening secularism. The world around us still finds Christ's followers hard to fathom; giving their money away, caring for those they don't know, loving people who don't care. Why do they do this? It's all too different, and here, in the difference, is the truth: it's the care and love Jesus shares with us that we too can share with the world. What the world counts as folly or madness, God counts as work well done.

Consider these...

To be me, there must be a time when I am only me, separate, away from the one I love and who loves me, alone in my world where no one else may enter in. That private place I do not share, perhaps could never share with you, not even you. I wanted to, but you wouldn't listen. I tried, but you wouldn't care. So often, I wished to speak, to say, to share – so often. Did you care? My world cried, I cried inside, around me parties happened. My world felt pain, there you sat in joy. My world is private. Tell me, do you still love me, even if you do not know my world, the world I will never let you enter?

The woman sitting between the crowds – is she the loneliest person? Is it by choice or circumstance? Her choice or mine? Is it her circumstance, or one I've made for her? She chose, did she? How can we tell?

The man in the corner, "always in the corner" they later said. Never spoke much. Just in the corner, sitting, watching. We never spoke. He never said. Just in the corner – his name? Sorry, I never asked.

She looks at our world, sees what we're doing, sees us all, but only ever sees. I never noticed or saw her. She's gone you say. Sorry.

Jesus too is sitting in a corner, alone and uncared for amongst the crowds who couldn't care less about Him, wishing someone would reach out and say hello.

And there's us ...we're there too, somewhere, if we look carefully. Are we just looking, or did we say hello?

Ignoring the World, Part One
By ignoring the world, we remain inside our own self made world, behind our bolted doors, oblivious to the cries of the afflicted (Psalm 9:12). Whatever happens, it's not my problem, not me. I did not cause the quake, flood, or sinking. I'm not responsible. It wasn't me. I am alone and safe.

Another Ignoring
Proverbs is a book most people have dipped in and out of, just for a look so they can say they have. It's a strange book – not sure about reading all of it. It's said to be the thoughts of King Solomon, or perhaps another writer. Solomon the King is famed for his judgment on squabbling women and baby halves. My favourite Solomon story is the Queen of Sheba's visit (1 Kings 10).

She arrives stuffed to the gunwales with gifts fit for a King (well she would, wouldn't she). Amongst the gold and precious stones she presents Solomon with several tons of almug wood. Nice gift, good for DIY, but there's just so much of it.

Almug trees are a pleasant smelling reddish hard wood, which King Solomon uses as temple and palace pillars, and the rest for musical instruments – versatile stuff. Out of all his gifts, it's the almug wood which gets centre stage – support with beauty. The pillars stood, supporting the roof for just over 360 years, whilst becoming part of the furniture. I wonder how soon people stopped saying, "Hey Almug wood, mmmmm ... good stuff," and how quickly they became just pillars.

As we look around our world, have the needs of our world, present for so long, become just another feature of the landscape? We've seen them so often, frequently crying out, asking for our concern: the envelopes in the post, the plastic bags for collections, the boxes asking for our pennies. All too soon the suffering becomes familiar. All too soon it is forgotten in the routines of our lives.

When we look around our homes, even at the most beautiful things we possess, a moment comes (or will come soon) when they are just there, almost invisible. The precious vase will lose its centre place, to be replaced with a fine cut bowl, itself usurped by a painting glittering bright, which fades as we now look upon our nice new antique ... Slowly, over time, we become used to it. The vase is sitting on the window sill now, sporting a bunch of dying flowers. No longer the central attraction, it's just there, there un-noticed, it's become background.

The Final Ignore

As we look around, what do we see, really see? Around us there are many pieces of background: objects, places, gifts, people, needs, ideas, smells, wants, desires, almug wood, Jesus.

> "Lord, when did we see you hungry and feed you, or thirsty and give you something to drink? When did we see you a stranger and invite you in, or needing clothes and clothe you? When did we see you sick or in prison and go to visit you?" The King will reply, "I tell you the truth, whatever you did for one of the least of these brothers of mine, you did for me" (Matthew 25:37-40).

At the end of the world, there will be Jesus, and He's asking a question to each and every member of the planet:

> "When I was hungry, when I was in need, when I was an outcast, when I was part of the background, were you there? What did you do?"

What are we going to do about it, or is this now just background?

Prayer

Father, teach me to see the world through your eyes. Help me to see its wonder and beauty, refreshed each day. Teach me to see the needs of your world, also refreshed each day. Help me not to ignore them or see them as background. Help me to see them as a need that I should be doing something about. Amen.

Memory verse

Psalm 51:10

Create in me a pure heart, O God, and renew a steadfast spirit within me.

Action

As you shop, go to the library, the leisure centre, or hang out in the precinct, consider the people around you, their lives, wants and needs. Now think of the needs being met where you live, through community centres, drop-ins, community groups, charity shops or similar. How could you get involved, how could you make a difference? Go and find just one group and see if you could support them in some way.

Day 12

The six step care dance - steps to follow

Reading: John 15:16-17

[16] You did not choose me, but I chose you and appointed you to go and bear fruit - fruit that will last. Then the Father will give you whatever you ask in my name. [17] This is my command: Love each other.

Meditation

Standing in a line waiting to be chosen; now there's two remaining; who's going to be last? What if we're never chosen, what if the game starts and we're still standing there un-chosen, what then? My gifts and skills become wasted to the game and my team is outnumbered and beaten, all because I was not chosen. I could've been so good, but no one noticed me. I was abandoned to the waiting line of life, alone. This is not so with dancing as it takes two to dance. It's fun to watch, exhausting to do, and comes with steps. Steps help adjust our minds to recalling what's coming next. Without knowing where we're going, we arrive there unnoticed. As with dancing, so with life, guidance allows us to see gaps between our knowledge.

God's choices are perfect for the tasks, with many of us being picked numerous times for different roles in our lifetimes. God is not, as J H Newman comments, looking for perfection. Newman said, "A man would do nothing if he waited until he could do it so well that no one could find fault." This is true of God. If He waited till we thought we were ready, we'd sit on the bench till we died. God chooses us when we're ready, whether we think we're ready or not.

To get to that chosen moment takes effort and training on our part, watched over by a diligent coach, God our Father, who corrects gently, goading our actions into greatness. Like many athletes, God's training schedules run against the trends of our natural world. Our world seeks status, power, money, influence. Our God seeks love, care, concern, and understanding. Our God requires examination of our life's direction, where we've gone so far, so that we may change tack to align ourselves with God's ways. Our world screams we must have what the world can offer, to the cost of everyone in it.

What if we don't like where we're sent, the task we're picked for? Can we change suburbs, continents? Callings / missions / sendings / instructions – whatever comes from God may be either life-long or 'for a season'. What is noticeable is that God prepares and readies us for His tasks. Jesus' disciples were not sent out in pairs until they'd received training and demonstrations on what to do (basic evangelism seminars, giving your conversion testimony in less than 100 words, how to shake dust from your sandals – that sort of thing). Saying to God, "Can I change," may have some dire consequences.

Wherever we're placed, it's for a reason. Occasionally we may be unsure whether what we're doing is right. We may never get to know till our time there ends, when the season's finished. Like trees and plants, we cannot say, "I'm off," as our roots are stuck in the garden till God chooses to transplant us.

Preparation, nurturing, challenging, is God style, as He lovingly and gently carves us into who we can really be for Him. Well, mostly. It's not always a gentle process. Jonah is swallowed by a large amphibious creature and spewed up on the beach. Daniel is dropped into the lion's den for a bit of one-on-one. For each of us (and them) there is careful moulding somewhere. For Jonah, it was running away – then he met his big fish. Without his big fish, Jonah wouldn't have been prepared, or even got as far as Nineveh.

Daniel only met and got to know his lions following the trickery by King Darius' advisers. Not life directions either Jonah or Daniel would have chosen.

Occasionally changes in life direction are very strange. Failing exams everyone thought we'd ace; being sent to a new posting by mistake; a chance conversation on the underground; going to a college we never would've picked; reading that odd book we've been given. The unexpected is God all over. He's the master of the unexpected. Indeed, the unexpected never is unexpected for Him, as He's planned it all for us. We just have to agree to go and do it, as Jonah found out. And we arrive there wondering, "How on earth did I get to do that? That's amazing, I'd never have thought of doing that, but it was so right, just for me, spot on."

If we let God work in our lives, our lives shift. We're picked from the waiting line of life and transformed. We may not always like where we are (in the fish or chatting to the lions), but there's a purpose in it. It's God's training camp, God's work, which comes in many forms.

Working with God is about people and attitudes. Most people crave to be known by someone, touched by them, or have someone somewhere who knows them reasonably well. Getting to know someone can be quite challenging. I'm not sure if I can trust you. What if I tell you that and you hate me? I could never say that to you, but I want to. Listening and accepting what's said can be quite hard, as another's thoughts often trigger bits of self recognition in us – "Mmmmmm that's me too." And here is God at work, changing not just one life, but many lives through ours.

Being chosen means listening too. Listening is made up of four parts. Firstly, active listening – not just sitting there passively accepting what they say. Secondly, taking time to know them, not as the other half of someone we already know. Thirdly, understanding them for what they hold close and base their life on, irrespective of what we may think about it. Lastly, feeling their anguish at the world, their joy and excitement, and the discoveries of God's world that they share with us, changing how we see God's world.

We're placed here and tasked by God with a purpose, only because He knows we're ready and able. We're never given anything outside our capabilities, even though at the time it may seem exactly like that.

To help us with God's tasks we're given the same power the disciples had (Luke 9 – Jesus sends them out with power). Isaiah says of this: "...the Lord will renew their strength, they will soar on wings like eagles, they will run and not grow weary, they will walk and not be faint" (Isaiah 40:30-31). With the Holy Sprit's help we do.

Of course, standing in the line of life, waiting to be picked, does not mean we actually have to accept the picking. We're free to stay in the line, waiting; waiting as the game starts, the plays are made, goals scored, victories won. We don't have to join in, not until were ready or till God sends a big fish or some lions.

Prayer

Father, help me to use what you have given me. Help me to reach inside for strength when I need to step out and be of service. Show me how you would have me live my life for others, and not always for myself. Let me be your hands and feet, your hugs and care to your world. Amen.

Memory verse

Amos 5:24

But let justice roll on like a river, righteous like a never failing stream!

Action

Ask a friend to sum up your life for you. Ask them to be honest as they and you feel you can cope with. Ask them whether they believe that you are in the right job, geographical place, doing the right things in your life. Pray over the results, asking God to illuminate any changes that might need to be made.

Day 13

Dance one: Listening

Reading: Luke 23:39-43

³⁹ One of the criminals who hung there hurled insults at him: "Aren't you the Christ? Save yourself and us!" ⁴⁰ But the other criminal rebuked him. "Don't you fear God," he said, "since you are under the same sentence? ⁴¹ We are punished justly, for we are getting what our deeds deserve. But this man has done nothing wrong." ⁴² Then he said, "Jesus, remember me when you come into your kingdom." ⁴³ Jesus answered him, "I tell you the truth, today you will be with me in paradise."

Meditation

Who was the last person to give you that 'unlistened to' look? The silent stare piled high with, "Where's my answer? You weren't listening were you? And whatever you say next, whatever it is, it had better be good and have, 'I love you' in it, or else…!"

Jesus is a very good listener, even before and after He died. If hanging on a cross is not distraction enough, Jesus takes time out to listen, do some pastoral work, die, and redeem us all.

A question sometimes posed which challenges our listening is: where do we listen best? Is it when we are seated in the side-by-side and slightly angled armchairs? Is it in the confrontational head on stance? Is it when we are more relaxed in bed with the light out kind of thing? Is it when we're just going out the door in a hurry? Or is it none of the above?

Hanging on His cross, Jesus demonstrates to us that the most useful type of listening is usually done in the most uncomfortable places, and often at the most awkward times. Why? Because we're not the ones who have the 'something I've just got to say to you right now, it'll just take a second,' or that look of 'help me.' Fail to listen and the moment's lost, time passes and another lost opportunity. On the cross Jesus didn't say, "Look, can't this wait, I'm dying here. You've had all this time, why now?" We see the Saviour of the world with His dying breath still seeking to save the lost (Luke 19:10).

The time to listen is often right now, no matter what we're doing, even dying. Now is the right time. All we see of the person is their outside. If we knew their inside, we'd have stopped and listened long ago. We'd have stayed and listened, not speaking. We'd be quiet until they finished, and only then say, "How may I help you," and "Jesus loves you."

Notice how Jesus, hanging on His cross, 'listens' to both arguments from the other two hanging there. Despite being in the same position as them, we find Jesus listening with compassion. Even nailed to a cross, love and care flow from Him. He is never too busy to care. The other cruxifixees clearly see He's God – no half way measures. "Aren't you the Christ?" they ask. "Save yourself and us!" Some translations have this thief blaspheming Jesus. The Greek text uses the word βλασφημέω, pronounced 'blasfaymeho', which has come to mean speaking irreverently about God. The word Luke uses is more to rile, or to speak reproachfully. Whatever the translation, we have both the other cruxifixees asking Jesus to do something, albeit with different intentions. Jesus does what He always does, offering hope where forgiveness is sought: "Today you will be with me in paradise."

As he dies, Jesus listens and comforts. He does not interrupt or say, "Have you considered this ...?" or "What's your view on ...?" He is silent, listening. Listening is stilling our minds, not thinking of our response, but allowing time for the other person to say what's on their heart. Only then should we think of how we should respond. It's giving the other person our time, all of it in Jesus' case.

I'm told that when you're on a cross it's rather hard to breathe, let alone have protracted conversations. Both crucifixees have quite long discussions with Jesus under the circumstances. Just breathing is a matter of pushing up onto the nails through your feet. The importance of those short phrases to them was huge, as breathing and speaking involved such pain. What they had to say at that moment was vital. It could not wait. Literally, it really could not wait.

Jesus' only reply is one of compassion and hope: "I tell you the truth, today you will be with me in paradise."

It's never too late for Jesus' forgiveness, even hanging on your cross. Thankfully most of us will never be nailed to a cross, but it doesn't remove the crosses from our lives. For example, those moments when we're so busy, our lives buzzing with congestion, and someone asks, "Could I have a word, I've …?" We are told to take up our cross and follow Jesus. In the busyness of daily life, when life itself becomes our cross, consider Jesus listening, comforting, forgiving, and having time for others, even whilst nailed to a large heavy wooden cross.

Listening for many is hard. It's its own skill. We're so used to thinking through the lines of conversations, sometimes we may just forget the other person's there, asking us to listen, not just to be present. Active listening requires out attention to what's being said, how it's said, and particularly what's missed out. It also needs us to monitor ourselves as we listen, noting our reactions to what's said, just as lawyers listen intently to witnesses' replies, only then considering their next question.

What makes a good listener? It depends. A good listener is usually someone who's worked out how to sit and hear the words, the silences and tears; someone who listens to what another has to say, without judgment or cause to interrupt, with no malice or issue in relation to what's being said. There is no agenda, but freedom, with time and space to listen – just as Jesus listens.

What does listening look like in practice (besides hanging on a cross)? It's seeing what makes a barrier – what stops someone saying whatever they will. Such as advising when no advice is asked for, or suggesting too soon, or reassuring without seeing if that's what's really needed, or disagreeing and blaming instead of being quiet. Such are the things we place between us and the voice yearning for someone to be quiet and listen.

Our walk with listening is one of observing our non-verbal behaviour, developing an awareness of how others see us, allowing silences, reflecting feelings, paraphrasing, probing gently with carefully constructed questions, and giving encouragement with little "Mmmmmms." These help us to hear and comfort, as we too would wish to be comforted in our own need.

Jesus asks only that we try and listen, and through this care for the needs of those who right now just need to say…

Prayer

Father, help me to be as your Son Jesus is, one with a listening ear upon whom many may come and share their burdens. Help me to stop myself from jumping in too fast, speaking my mind too quickly, when others just need someone to share with. Jesus, thank you for your example of listening as you died on the cross. Help me to be like you, as you listen to the world. I also pray that, in my turn, someone will be a listening ear for me and for my concerns. Amen.

Memory verse

Luke 19:10

For the Son of Man came to seek and to save what was lost.

Action

Go and find a loved one, who you know and care for. Tell them that you've just been reading about listening, and that you want to put into practice what you've read. Spend about 10 minutes, listening to how they are, their day, what's been happening. And as they share, think about what they're saying, rather than how you would wish to answer what's being said.

Day 14

Dance two: Taking time to know them

Reading: Matthew 4:18-22

The Calling of the First Disciples

[18] As Jesus was walking beside the Sea of Galilee, he saw two brothers, Simon called Peter and his brother Andrew. They were casting a net into the lake, for they were fishermen. [19] "Come, follow me," Jesus said, "and I will make you fishers of men." [20] At once they left their nets and followed him.

[21] Going on from there, he saw two other brothers, James son of Zebedee and his brother John. They were in a boat with their father Zebedee, preparing their nets. Jesus called them, [22] and immediately they left the boat and their father and followed him.

Meditation

The girl sitting opposite me as I journey northwards on the underground is a stranger. In all likelihood I will never see her again. This is it, my only opportunity to know her. It's now or never. She too, has a choice of knowing me. If only we would speak, say hello. Who knows where it would lead? If I never say hello, I will never know her name, where she lives, what she does, her email, her likes and dislikes, her favourite iTunes – nothing at all. She will remain forever just a face opposite me.

    Jesus faces a similar situation on a Galilean shoreline. He needs to build a band of disciples willing at some future point to give away their very lives for the message He's going to give them. He needs to know them, and they him, with a 'knowing' that is very close indeed.

Jesus could have looked inside their heads and gone, "Yes, yes, yes ... no not you ... yes, you ... oh definitely not you!" Instead he takes the human route, getting to know them over time, a route which not only takes time but effort. For many of us, getting to know people is not easy. For some it's quite a painful experience, full of rejections, hurtful words, looks, and even a matter of reputation: "Oh don't talk to her, she's ..." For others it's a different story, with lots of friends, popularity, being the centre of the class, and also a matter of reputation: "Oh, do tell me where you got that from." As Jesus knows, both scenarios have a simple challenge at their centre, the challenge of letting others know us. But if I tell you who I am, will you like me, will you love me, will you want to look at me and talk with me? Please don't turn away. I'm sorry. I meant it to sound differently. That's not what I meant. I'm sorry, can we start again?

For some it's painful letting someone know them. The problem is, it's a two way road; I say something, you say something, and we get to know each other, getting closer each time. This may be chatting, flirting, looking, smiling, exchanging ideas, sharing thoughts, or just passing the time. Each encounter with the same person leaves an impression. Seeing them again, tells them more about me, and I get to know them more. Horrors, I wonder what they think! Am I getting to know you, or just flirting with you? How do I tell?

Knowing and being known is one of God's greatest gifts to us, but it is a gift that's frequently abused, often under-used, and certainly never fully explored. Take the Garden of Eden. There's Adam with Eve, and there's God, (unsure how many angels around at the time). Even after the eventful apple incident, there's still understanding, harsh but an understanding. You did this (apple eating), you can come to this point and no further (barred from the garden, no re-entry!), do you understand Me?

Likewise King David when confronted by his transgression sees himself for what he really is. Wailing loudly, as Psalm 51 records, he cries out to God for compassion. Job is similarly unhappy with God, choosing to attempt a world record humble pie eating challenge. Each of them was known to themselves (eventually) and to those around them for their actions. And being known by others was the healing catalyst in their lives.

The experience of each of these people (and the Bible spills over with such incidents) is in all of us: seeing where we've been, what we've done, and realising we've made a mess again. We need someone like Jesus, someone trusted enough to say that thing we could never say to anyone, the friend who is just being a friend, not actually saying anything at the moment, because we're doing all the talking – a friend who is there for us. Jesus modelled such a friendship during his earthly life, leaving the Holy Spirit to be with us for all time, so we are never truly alone, being there when it matters.

However, the Bible records that, strange though it might seem, Jesus was not always present when there was a need during His earthly life; for example, Jairus' daughter (Mark 5), the widow's son (Luke 7), Lazarus (John 11). Why was Jesus absent? – Essentially because He wasn't there. During His time on earth He obeyed the rules (almost all the time), the earthly ones. There was only one of Him. He could only be in one place at a time. He does arrive to heal and comfort, showing he cares, even though he was not there at the time, just as we should do when we arrive following a loss or a tragedy. When Jesus is there, he takes the initiative, showing compassion, getting to know them, and finding out what's going on, what's needed.

The cost of knowing someone, and of someone knowing you, is not enormous. The enormity is in the first question: "Hello, I'm..., and you're...?" If we keep doing this, sharing and accepting more from each other each time we meet, we come to share the greatest of gifts: friendship. And for some, this blossoms into love, still within a friendship.

Jesus doesn't expect us to get to know everyone (there's not enough time) – just a few people, to make a few differences in the world. What does this look like in practice?

- Listening to me, when I need to do all the talking
- Respecting me and my feelings – not putting them down
- Understanding me, my feelings, moods, tantrums, lies, and issues
- Helping me (this might not always be them solving the problem)
- Loving me unconditionally, without prejudice or judgment
- Disagreeing with me, yet still wanting to stay next to me
- Telling me I should change what I'm wearing because it doesn't go with anything else on the planet (alive, dead, or yet to come)
- Sitting in the car next to me and not needing to talk to each other – just being together
- Praying for me when I'm not there
- Caring for me, even after what I've said and done
- Forgiving me for the above (no matter how many 'aboves' there are)
- Trusting me enough to trust them in what I say to them
- Giving me space to be me, even when I'm wearing that top (again)
- Helping me to change into what I can become, with gentle challenges and encouragements

- Allowing me to be me, and helping me to share with them the me I cannot face inside

Who are you being friends with today? We can always just smile at the girl on the underground and say, "Hello, I'm ... and you're ...?"

Prayer

Father, help me to be a friend to your world, to those around and near to me, to those I love and those who love me, to those I meet as I journey through your world. Help me especially to be a friend to those who see themselves as unloveable, those whom the world has hurt, those whom the world has rejected, and those for whom love and care are strangers. Amen.

Memory verse

Matthew 4:19

"Come, follow me," Jesus said, "and I will make you fishers of men."

Action

Look around at your work, your office, factory, school, shop, the place you meet for groups. Who do you see and who do you not know? Who sits on the edge, finds it hard to join the conversations, and is perhaps longing to even just be called by their name? Go and say "Hello, I'm ... and you're ...?"

Day 15

Dance three: Warning against refusing God

Reading: Hebrews 12:15-25

[15] See to it that no one misses the grace of God and that no bitter root grows up to cause trouble and defile many.

[25] See to it that you do not refuse him who speaks. If they did not escape when they refused him who warned them on earth, how much less we will, if we turn away from him who warns us from heaven.

Meditation

Why is it even necessary for the writer of Hebrews to remind his readers to make sure no one's missing out on God's grace? What's happened? Obviously something has. The Bible gives many similar informative warnings, and describes the consequences of not helping those in need. Frequently these are preludes to crunch moments, giving hearers time to change their minds before 'it's now too late' arrives.

The writer gives a descriptive choice: are they refusers or ignorers? In refusing something, be it presents, people or God, they really need to know what they're refusing, and the consequences. Without such understanding, they're merely ignorers, never having understood or experienced what they're refusing. Our world abounds with ignorers, those who say, "They don't matter", "I'm not interested", "If I walk by on the other side of the road, no one will know, honest!" unless Jesus makes a parable about them that is.

Ignoring comes with few attachments and little need to understand. Thankfully true ignorers are quite rare. We're an inquisitive bunch. We just have to go and have a look, or at least slow down as we drive past the accident. It's no use pretending people don't know what's happening, which is the Hebrew writer's point. They do, they understand what's going on, but hey, let's look the other way. No one's watching, right? No one cares, right? Someone does, and then the crunch moment is upon them.

If we do not care for others, why should we care for ourselves? But we do. We care quite passionately about ourselves. We watch out for ourselves every time. I've got to have that dress, that car, that DVD; I must go and see … ; I need to have that … ! I just got to, you understand! Amongst all our materialism, have we inadvertently become refusers or ignorers? Are we refusing others needs, or are just ignoring them?

Knowing what's good for someone brings us to a decision. If we know what's good for us, why do we sometimes deny this same goodness to someone else? Why are they missing out, when we don't? Who put us in charge of the 'You Miss Out Department'? Why are we letting others miss out on the grace of God when we know it's good for them? Don't worry if this sounds a little harsh. The writer to the Hebrews was actually writing about these same issues.

Sometimes we don't realise that we have to do something, or that the responsibility is ours.

Are we being hypocritical? Probably not. Hypocrisy comes in several guises, as Matthew 23:25 shows with the Pharisees. Jesus here is 'outing' them. He says, "… You clean the outside of the cup and dish, but inside they are full of greed and self-indulgence." They understand what should be done, but refuse, only doing what is good for them. Are we that selfish? Probably not. Are we really just watching out for us every time?

Perhaps not every time, but under our surface lurks a selfish passion, in need of control and tempering.

It would only take the Pharisees a moment to reach out and care, but that's it, they don't. Eye contact is hard enough, smiling is out of the question, so talking and caring for someone just isn't going to happen.

For many of us, it's quite hard sometimes to make initial contact and ask if we may help. We see someone struggling. Inside we know we should at least say hello, and then a quick "May I help?" hoping they're OK. For many others it's a question of what to do after I've said hello. I'm not really a conversationalist. I can't keep saying hello. There has to be conversation. HELP! Jesus, recognising this conundrum, sent His disciples out in pairs, so they could support each other when they went somewhere new. Like them we need support. If we're with our friend, saying "Hello, may I help?" to someone is a little less frightening.

Think of the first time you tried something new with someone – lots of 'what ifs'. What if they don't like it? What if I don't like it? What do I say? How do I refuse? Will it be fun or painful? What if that happened? Should I ...?

We survived. Our friends still talk to us, if perhaps a little differently having shared an experience together. Nothing catastrophic happened. The world still trundled on, spinning round the sun! It may be slightly more battered in places, but we're still here.

We know how to talk and to be with our friends. We know how to comfort them, because we understand them, and they us. The writer here challenges us to take this a little further, by watching out for others. The original Greek text has the word, 'τις' (pronounced 'tis') meaning 'someone' or 'a certain one'. It's this person the writer calls us to care for, using all the communication skills, care, and support tactics we already know and use with our friends. We understand how to make new friends. It's only because we occasionally forget to jump outside our comfort zone we don't meet others who we could care for.

Preparing to care is about being equipped. The most vital part of this preparation is prayer. No leaping into action without first prayers. Through prayer we can ask God how He would have us care. We may have many ideas, but only God knows what they really need. Sometimes it is just our prayers, not an actual going and doing. By not doing, we're not ignoring or refusing God's intervention in their lives, but we're being guided by God as to what is best for them, which is frequently more useful and productive.

Unlike the recipients of the Letter to the Hebrews, we know what God is like and the love He would have us share, understanding that we should be caring for His world.

As we look around, perhaps as the writer to the Hebrews did, what do we see? Sitting next to us, a young couple argues. Opposite is the man who needs to sleep off whatever he's had. Along from us, a lady is crying. Us? We're sitting here and the crunch moment has arrived.

Prayer

Father, thank you for placing me here next to these people. I pray for them, for all their needs, both seen and unseen. Help and guide me in how you would use me, right here and now, to show your care. Amen.

Memory verse

Hebrews 12:15

See to it that no one misses the grace of God...

Action

Look around you, as you travel, as you sit, as you walk around. Who do you see? What are their needs? Pray for five totally new people you've never prayed for before. It might not be by name. It could be the person you met in the shops today, or the new person at work.

Day 16

Dance four: Release from suffering

Reading: John 21:15-17

Jesus Reinstates Peter

¹⁵ When they had finished eating, Jesus said to Simon Peter, "Simon son of John, do you truly love me more than these?" "Yes, Lord," he said, "you know that I love you." Jesus said, "Feed my lambs." ¹⁶ Again Jesus said, "Simon son of John, do you truly love me?" He answered, "Yes, Lord, you know that I love you." Jesus said, "Take care of my sheep." ¹⁷ The third time he said to him, "Simon son of John, do you love me?" Peter was hurt because Jesus asked him the third time, "Do you love me?" He said, "Lord, you know all things; you know that I love you." Jesus said, "Feed my sheep."

Meditation

What makes us suffer? Cancer, brain tumours, paralysis, dementia, blindness, mental health issues, and so the list continues. Each brings suffering, for us, our patients, carers, anyone we know.

When someone dies at home and an ambulance is called, they provide a pack called 'Helpful Information Following Bereavement'. Not something expected, but valued. It ends by suggesting that you may wish to seek help or to share your emotions before the loneliness arrives.

Research suggests the best place to be alone is sitting in a pub at around 3pm. No one notices you, no one cares – total invisibility. The world around is busy with itself, doing its utmost to ignore you. You could die and it would take maybe an hour for anyone to notice. Try it (maybe not the dying). Go and sit in an unfamiliar pub, cafe, library, wherever, and see what happens. Once you're served, the world moves away becoming no longer interested in you. Sitting alone, no matter where, reminds us of an emptiness which exists a moment's breath from each of us. What if no one was at home to say, "Hi, how's your day?" or "Be there – by the way, it's your turn to cook" or "Why are you late?" At least someone's there. Consider someone for whom this emptiness is usual. There is no one else in their lives. Do we notice them sitting there? Are they too ashamed or too alone? Is there too much going on in their life to share it? Or maybe nothing much happens for them, and they would like a life to share.

Jesus too knew the pain of loneliness, as when He wept over the death of Lazarus (John 11:35). Alone with His thoughts, His humanity was uncovered – His own humanity that could not be repressed as He shared the pain experienced by Mary at the loss of her brother. As our God, Jesus would have known He was going raise Lazarus, but none the less He wept.

Observe Peter when he denies he knows Jesus. Peter's reaction to his own denial is utter despair. He could do little more to hurt someone. In denying Jesus he disowns his very self, realising how contemptible he's become. Going outside, he weeps uncontrollably, engulfed by his emotions and his actions. He's no longer Peter the rock on which the church is founded. He's the small child crying for the words he never meant to say, hoping no one's there to notice – crying where no comfort may enter, no further thoughts beyond the next set of racking tears. The world has truly ended for him, there is no more.

We're not told what happens to Peter immediately after. We next meet him when Jesus asks him three times if he loves Him. Peter now is quite hurt. You can see it running through his mind: "Why is Jesus asking if I love Him again. I told Him didn't I? What more does He want?" Jesus asks Peter three times, as He wants Peter's suffering to cease. Jesus, the healer, draws out Peter's pain, releasing him from his suffering.

Jesus' earthly ministry was to a people surrounded by oppression, hate, and fear: oppression from the Roman invaders, hate from surrounding nations, fear from the numerous internal political and religious struggles. Jesus sees all of this and shares the pain. Releasing suffering and freeing those held captive by it – this is Jesus' trademark. He doesn't want a world held prisoner in misery and affliction.

Jesus craves to make a difference, wishing people to know Him more and experience His healing. We may decide to come, or we can make our excuses. Whichever it is, He still loves us, healing when we ask and not before, never imposing, always waiting. "Come to me, all you who are weary and burdened, and I will give you rest" (Matthew 11:28). All four Gospels record crowds flocking to Jesus, jostling, touching, seeking Him out for care. He sends out His own disciples to care for and heal the world around them, and poses a question to us: will you go and do likewise?

Doubters say no one's actually healed today, it's really just emotions. For sceptics, please go and see for yourself. Talk to one of the thousands alive today who have been physically touched and healed by Jesus. And yet we fear to come to Jesus for healing, because there's that question – what if we're not healed?

What if I'm not healed from my suffering? What if it continues? Why me? Why are some healed and others not? Why me? We do not know why suffering continues. Here, as in no other place, is where we need to care. It's easy to celebrate release from suffering, but it can be harder to comfort those who are still suffering. It really is here that we need to care. Holding the almost weightless hand of someone dying, looking into their eyes and seeing the pain looking back. Jesus, why did you not heal them? Help me to care. I'm all out of strength and energy here. Jesus, do something.

On several occasions the prophet Isaiah speaks of renewed strength, strength to live in a world full of oppression, hate, and fear – an oppression imposed by world powers, a hate from warring nations, a fear from political powerlessness – a suffering world itself in need of care.

The question of why some are healed and other not remains unanswered – a question for Jesus.

The fear of failure, of no healing, is strong in most of us. We don't like it 'not to work'. Such a fear may occasionally prevent someone seeking out ways of changing their life, making friends, or asking for healing. Fears do not always arise from inside us. Jesus reminds us that this world is still locked in mortal combat with the devil. New look, same tricks – trying to conquer the world, spreading deceit as freely as raindrops, deceiving the world, telling people, "You're in control, you don't need help, you can do it alone." And look where it gets us. The world seems to have turned against itself, growing up into a rebellious teenager. And like teenagers they are trying to do it their own way. Just like teenagers did before them (Well we did, didn't we? The looks, the clothes, those shoes, and "You're not going out the house dressed like that!").

Despite the continuing pain and suffering, Jesus still cares. He asks of us, as He did Peter, three questions, as He seeks to find what we can give. For some this is much, for others a little less, and for some it's smaller. Look at John 21:15-17 and Jesus' response to Peter: "Feed my lambs … Take care of my sheep … Feed my sheep." Why the difference? They're all odd little woolly things aren't they? Well actually no, as Jesus points out to Peter. Lambs are ready to feed from anyone, but caring for sheep requires a bit more experience, whilst feeding a sheep demands specific care and attention. So it depends on what Jesus wants us to do. Some are called to care generally, others to tackle specific demands, whilst others are tasked with more complex roles and ministries.

Is Jesus calling you to do something?

Prayer

Father, help me to see how and where you would have me serve you, and what role and ministry you are shaping for me. Use me in your service to care for your people, wherever the need is. Amen.

Memory verse

John 1:1

In the beginning was the Word, and the Word was with God, and the Word was God.

Action

Go through your address book, phone contacts, friends, and other contacts, looking for two or three people who you know may be suffering. Book a time to go and see them. Pray with them, take them out somewhere special, or sit and hold their hand – whatever need they have. This may be the beginning of your new ministry.

Day 17

Dance five: The devil and all that stuff

Readings

1 Peter 5:8-9

⁸ Be self-controlled and alert. Your enemy the devil prowls around like a roaring lion looking for someone to devour. ⁹ Resist him, standing firm in the faith, because you know that your brothers throughout the world are undergoing the same kind of sufferings.

James 4:1-12

Submit Yourselves to God

⁴ What causes fights and quarrels among you? Don't they come from your desires that battle within you? ² You want something but don't get it. You kill and covet, but you cannot have what you want. You quarrel and fight. You do not have, because you do not ask God. ³ When you ask, you do not receive, because you ask with wrong motives, that you may spend what you get on your pleasures. ⁴ You adulterous people, don't you know that friendship with the world is hatred toward God? Anyone who chooses to be a friend of the world becomes an enemy of God. ⁵ Or do you think Scripture says without reason that the spirit he caused to live in us envies intensely? ⁶ But he gives us more grace. That is why Scripture says: "God opposes the proud but gives grace to the humble." ⁷ Submit yourselves, then, to God. Resist the devil, and he will flee from you. ⁸ Come near to

God and he will come near to you. Wash your hands, you sinners, and purify your hearts, you double-minded. [9] Grieve, mourn and wail. Change your laughter to mourning and your joy to gloom. [10] Humble yourselves before the Lord, and he will lift you up. [11] Brothers, do not slander one another. Anyone who speaks against his brother or judges him speaks against the law and judges it. When you judge the law, you are not keeping it, but sitting in judgment on it. [12] There is only one Lawgiver and Judge, the one who is able to save and destroy. But you—who are you to judge your neighbour?

Meditation

Devil: Myth or Reality

The man in the street (or the lawyer on the Clapham omnibus) if questioned over the devil often says he's more myth than reality, perhaps adding a strange story they've heard. Unfortunately, the same question to some Christians produces similar results: "He's in the Bible isn't he?"

If unbelievers tell stories about the devil, why are some Christians almost ignoring him? Is it perhaps in case he's noticed, or is it that what they noticed is so fearful? Satan, the devil, Beelzebub, that one, is usually portrayed in the media as a charming kind of guy, with (or without) tail, with just a few unpleasant social habits. He's not that bad, just misunderstood? Jesus is very firm about the devil's role in what's going on, revealing him as the big deceiver. If you want to be had, he's your man, every time.

It's said that the surer someone is that they're being influenced, the more they'll try to hide it. Take advertising for instance. Back in the 1970s the British public was deprived of TV adverts during several weeks of television strikes. No TV, no entertainment. What did we do? We carried out research instead. During these strikes, studies found that we actually shopped less, quite dramatically less. Everyone knew TV adverts affected us, but not that much – the results were a little shocking. The majority of the major household names found their sales dropping during strikes; no adverts resulted in almost no customers. Surely this can't be right, we're not that gullible. Unfortunately, further television strikes revealed we are. If we're not repeatedly being told to buy something, we don't. Although most people, when questioned, said they just didn't fancy shopping.

Shopping is one thing, hiding or denying who influences and affects our lives, is more serious. As with the devil, being aware of how he affects us is important. Peter writes about this very idea when he says, "Be self-controlled and alert. Your enemy the devil prowls around like a roaring lion looking for someone to devour" (1 Peter 5:8).

CS Lewis captures some of our attitudes towards the devil. In the preface to his book 'Letters from a Senior to a Junior Devil' he writes about two errors people make in relation to the devil and demons. Firstly, we may disbelieve in him, and secondly, we may have, '...an excessive and unhealthy interest in them.' Evidently to CS Lewis, the devil's themselves are, '...equally pleased by both errors...' As the devil is the ultimate liar, everything that flows from deceit excites him. CS Lewis also points out that there is more than one devil, alluding to whole armies of demons all intent on destroying mankind. In his book, a junior devil called Wormwood is charged with guiding his human into the kingdom of Hell. The book ends with Wormwood being scolded by a senior devil for losing his human. He says of the human, 'There was a sudden clearing of his eyes (was there not?) as he saw you for the first time, and recognised the part you had had in him ...'

James knew just how the devil tries to deceive, often hiding from us. He writes, "Submit yourselves, then, to God. Resist the devil, and he will flee from you. Come near to God and he will come near to you" (James 4:7).

These are clearly not hollow words. They speak of a reality hovering around us and just looking for an opportunity. James talks of resistance, with the devil fleeing from us. To stand up to him we need to understand how he influences us. Knowing what's going on is a start, as CS Lewis, James, and Peter point out. As James reminds us, we're open to constant influence from the devil, hence the necessity of being on our guard. Guarding can be difficult, but it comes with practice and the help of God's Holy Spirit.

There is yet another side. We may know or suspect what's affecting us, yet chose to ignore it. It feels better and less threatening. If I convince myself I don't know, how much can it harm me? (Pause at this point whilst listening to the devil's laughter). To him deceit is the happiest moment. Unwittingly or not, another person falls into his trap. He's very good at traps, having had millenniums of practice.

We have a choice as to what to do about the devil:

- See what's going on and do nothing
- Ignore what's happening hoping it'll go away
- Decide we've had enough of his deceits and say to the devil, "Flee! I see you as you are."

Making a decision in those circumstances is where many people are most affected by the devil. He just does not want us to decide. By doing nothing we are kept in confusion, kept from doing the things we could be doing: loving, caring, helping, nurturing. The truth is that we could be freed from wasting time, wasting our energy, and wasting our very lives on worthless enterprises.

The devil is the great deceiver. To see him as anything less than this is inaccurate, as Jesus shows. Jesus' own reaction to the devil is always one of pointing out how ineffective he is before God, how in comparison to God the devil does not even come close. Instead of refuting this, the devil slinks away, looking for other opportunities.

James advises, "Resist the devil, and he will flee from you" (James 4:7). The devil fleeing? Well yes, he does, because he's seen for what he really is. No longer ignored, he's exposed to the light, which he cannot ever hope to overcome.

So what are we looking for, what do the fruits of the devil look like? Something like this:

- Lies and sin
- Wasted lives
- Torn apart families
- Hate and fear in our world
- War, famine, and pestilence
- Time stolen from us

What if that's me, or bits of me? What can I do about it? Pray for God's strength to stand up to the devil and the devil will flee. Go and find a friend to pray with about turning your life around and being filled with God's power, His Holy Spirit.

Jesus forgives whatever we've done, if we're sorry. So we get to start again each day – we get to have another go. Yesterday is forgotten. Today we can include Jesus in our lives and in the care we offer. Jesus, the devil's opposite, never lets us down. With him we can always make a difference. Jesus gives us the choice – the devil just pretends.

Prayer

Father, I pray for your power, your Holy Spirit, to fill me with your very self today. Help me to see areas of my life which are stopping me caring for those around me, areas that are stopping me making a difference in your world. Father, pray for your forgiveness where my life has strayed from your path. Restore me again, filling me with your love and care. Amen.

Memory verse

1 Peter 5:8

Be self-controlled and alert. Your enemy the devil prowls around like a roaring lion looking for someone to devour.

Action

Sit and think about what's gone on in your life over the last few days or the last week. Where have things gone wrong or not quite worked out? Is there anyone you've upset or got annoyed with? Go and make amends with them, praying for them and with them (if appropriate).

Day 18

Dance six: Jesus every time

Reading: Luke 9:23-27

²³ Then he said to them all: "If anyone would come after me, he must deny himself and take up his cross daily and follow me. ²⁴ For whoever wants to save his life will lose it, but whoever loses his life for me will save it. ²⁵ What good is it for a man to gain the whole world, and yet lose or forfeit his very self? ²⁶ If anyone is ashamed of me and my words, the Son of Man will be ashamed of him when he comes in his glory and in the glory of the Father and of the holy angels. ²⁷ I tell you the truth, some who are standing here will not taste death before they see the kingdom of God".

Meditation

Denying ourselves can seem a bit counter-productive. If God made us in His image, why deny ourselves? Are we not rejecting ourselves as God's creations? If we deny ourselves, what if we don't like what we find? As to taking up your cross daily, many would be hard pressed to identifying it. These are exactly Luke's points. Denying isn't supposed to be about rejecting me – it's about stepping outside me, my life, my wants; it's about turning around and seeing how I can help the person sitting next to me. This may then show us where our daily crosses are, through serving the needs of others. Daily crosses may come and go as God directs our lives. Finding them is about seeking God's direction for our lives. None of this should be done on our own. Jesus doesn't really want isolated Christians, doing their own thing. He calls us into His body, to work in harmony with each other, promoting His Kingdom by using all the gifts to care that He's given to each of us.

Going without is no easy ride. Our personal needs keep popping up, squashing our focus on where we believe God is leading us. We've got to say no to us sometimes, to give our life to our neighbour's needs, even if next door is several thousand miles away (such are Jesus' door arrangements). One day, we will bump into the rest of God's family in heaven, looking them in the eye as they ask us how we liked all the stuff we had whilst they had nothing. How difficult is it when someone asks, "Why did you not help me when I had a need? You had so much that you had to buy more cupboards just to store it all."

Denying is not an easy verb: "Do you really need another one of those? What's wrong with the one you have already?" Do we actually need this, or could we give it to someone who's in a better position to use it more effectively than us? (The man sleeping on the street without a coat is always in a better position than us, every time). God asks us to go without, not as a punishment or test, but because He loves us. Without His love in our lives, we would be down the shops spending endless amounts on us, as if tomorrow would never come. His love provides a controlling brake preventing us squandering ourselves, our time, our money on worthless things this world treasures. Today's new car is only tomorrow's rust – it's just waiting for oxidisation.

Given the choice, many of us would buy something, often just because it's there. Denying too is a choice, because we can choose not to; we're not obliged to buy something (just because it's there) and there's the difference. Jesus is very much into choices. We can let him into our lives, or not. We can choose to serve him, or not. We can choose to care for His world, or not. We can choose to deny ourselves things, or not. It's always our choice, no one else's. We can choose to care, or we can ignore the world. It's always our choice.

Many in our world claim to do good works, seeking to earn places in heaven through how much they do – their personal sacrifice. Good works they are, and the world is quite a better place with them. But without Jesus as instigator, they remain just good works. We can't earn our place in heaven, no matter how hard we try to deny ourselves. Ephesians 2:8-10 says that we are saved by God's grace, not by what we can do ourselves. No one can earn a place in heaven. It is a gift from God.

Denying comes with many complexities, as Titus discovers in Crete. Being good at something gets results. If we're good at something, God gives us another one to work on as Titus found. The ageing Titus is perhaps looking forward to a little rest, perhaps a nice nurturing church to work with, but instead he finds corruption, lies, and cheats, people leading others astray with their practices. Paul left Titus in Crete to, "...straighten out what was left unfinished..." (Titus 1:5). Thank you Paul! Titus' work with Paul at Ephesus shows that he is a tenacious leader, through his self sacrifice, his denying – the ideal man for a sticky church. Titus may have preferred a less trying task, but God saw in Titus whole vistas where he could really flourish with his Kingdom building. From Titus's results at Crete, we later find that he's moved onto a mission in Dalmatia. God (and Paul) would not have moved him on unless Crete was sorted.

Just after Titus is the book (ok, page) of Philemon. Onesimus! How wrong can you get it? Onesimus, having just stolen from Philemon, runs off. Paul writes, asking Philemon to take him back. You can imagine Philemon's initial reactions! ☹☹☹@Xx!??!!!!! Paul persuades him otherwise ☺. Onesimus, now a converted Christian wishes to return to his master. Sounds familiar? "But while he was still a long way off, his father saw him and was filled with compassion for him; he ran to his son, threw his arms around him, and kissed him" (Luke 15:20). As our loving Father, God only wants the best for us, no matter what we've done. Onesimus could so easily have hung around with Paul on another missionary journey. Deciding what was best for Onesimus, not for Paul, he sends him back to Philemon. In returning he risks death. Philemon is within his rights to have Onesimus killed for what he's done. Returning to where things have gone wrong and saying sorry can be very hard, but that is where he was supposed to be. That's sometimes where we're supposed to be, denying ourselves and denying our personal pride by serving there. Doing hard things is often where God places us, only because He knows we can do it with Him.

Some may think God is unkind placing us in difficult situations, seeing it almost as a punishment. But God only asks. He never pushes, and He knows that we cannot do it in our own strength alone. We have to rely on God's power and strength in doing it, but God only ever asks, nothing more. It's our choice, always our choice. The gifts He gives us are gifts of service, care, and love for others rather than for ourselves. Titus' leadership gift would never have blossomed if not honed on a 'rebellious people' (Titus 1:10). If we deny God's gifts by not using them, eventually they fade.

Sometimes in amongst the denying and self sacrifice we may have to acknowledge that the joy has gone from our lives, that our strength has waned, and that we need spiritual refreshment – God's love and comfort. Denying is about seeing what we need too. It's no good being worn out and denying everything in our own lives. This is not what God wants for us.

Jesus ask us as His followers, the ones He cares for deeply, to daily take up our cross for Him and to care for His people. It's our choice, always our choice.

Prayer

Father, help me to see what you would have me deny in my life, not what I feel I should be giving up for you. Help me to use what you have given me for your kingdom, so that others too may share in your blessings to me. Amen.

Memory verse

Colossians 3:2

Set your minds on above, not on earthy things.

Action

When was the last time you had a hunt through your clothes to see what you're still wearing and what's no longer useful to you? Do a clothes audit. If you find things you're no longer wearing, or things that are a bit small and you've not been able to get into them for a while, another person may value such items, as might a charity shop.

Day 19

Dance seven: Well there's always seven - have a rest as God did on the seventh day

Reading: Ephesians 5:15-20

[15] Be very careful, then, how you live - not as unwise but as wise, [16] making the most of every opportunity, because the days are evil. [17] Therefore do not be foolish, but understand what the Lord's will is. [18] Do not get drunk on wine, which leads to debauchery. Instead, be filled with the Spirit. [19] Speak to one another with psalms, hymns and spiritual songs. Sing and make music in your heart to the Lord, [20] always giving thanks to God the Father for everything, in the name of our Lord Jesus Christ.

Meditation

Lying in bed as the day begins. The waiting busy hustle screams "Come and get me!" before once more we arrive back between the sheets to sleep, and then start again tomorrow – another day, another hour of life. Today Sunday, is one of rest, and rest we should. We see relaxation littering the Gospels. Jesus sleeps. He takes time out to rest. His disciples rest (or more frequently fall asleep). We see times when Jesus, Peter, John, and many others, are chatting, discussing the world and where it's going, almost passing time, because they can. God rested. So too must we. Paul warns however, that no matter how we rest, we must be careful how we live, making the most of every opportunity.

One day, hopefully many, many, years from now, we will all lay dying. It has to come, unless Jesus makes it back first. For some, today is their last day. We may not know it, or even want to want to know it, but an end does come. If, and this is the question, if God granted you an extra 24 hours, what would you do with them?

We are reminded to live each day as if it was our last. If so, what's to be done, if today really is our very last day? Helping our neighbour, being with our family, writing down our precious thoughts, watching TV, resting? Whenever it turns out to be, at the end of the day, times up. What did you decide to do...?

As our 'deathday' is hopefully very far away, how should we live today? What about just this next hour? How important is this hour to you? How easily could we waste it, for it will never return? Will we spend it reading, writing, sleeping, watching the world go by, playing our favoured DVD, indulging in delicious food, being with friends, family, those with love, those we don't?

All are good. We can't be saving the planet all the time. Even God stopped for a break. What's important is what we 'do' with our hour. Doing nothing is a bit wasteful. We need a plan for what's in store, otherwise how do I know I've done it? Jesus planned, prepared, and considered what came next. So should we. One day, far from here, God is going to ask us what we did with our time, God's time. And our answer may be ... "Ermm, well it's like this ..." This hour, is it ours to throw away, or given as a gift to use wisely? If a gift, should I use it for you, me, or maybe both?

Paul writes to the Ephesians speaking of evil days. The devil still prowls around like a roaring lion seeking to devour, only now he's updated his tricks. Technology allows access to people, information, images, ideas, and websites – some enriching, others not so. Writers today publish books and articles actively seeking to remove God from our minds, as easily as sunlight falling to the earth. Society's moral base has shifted. No longer is it right or wrong. It's full of doing what's right for me (not you). Christians are still called to be salt, even if saltiness stings. Do we make a difference? If this is our last 24 hours, where's the difference we are making.

In creating our world, God had a purpose. Sometimes this may seem hard to believe, but it's there. It was a very large, expansive purpose. Otherwise why create our world? Our part is to understand this purpose, following how He would have us be as part of His plan. Just being here requires us to consider how we should live, without even getting started on the consequences of our actions.

Paul reminds the Ephesians about living, and the consequences of how we live, especially about drunkenness, which seems to be an issue. Being drunk does all sorts of things, mainly curtailing our own self control. Driving, walking, or even sitting becomes harder – talking is perhaps the worst! We lose control. What if that's our last 24 hours, being drunk somewhere?

How many of our actions are things which we'd be proud to say, "That's the last thing I did on earth"? The disciples faced such situations in which their actions did become their last acts on earth. Time and again they stood up and said, "Let me tell you about what Jesus has done in my life, about His love and care."

To be honest, we're never far from dying: hesitating in traffic, stepping off the bus, plugging in a light fitting, or just our own genetic makeup letting us down. What was the last thing I said, my very last words on earth? Did they cause pain, help someone, ease their suffering, hurt them? We do get to choose our last words, as the Coroner's courts show. They usually ask what the deceased was doing just beforehand. Frequently replies include what they said just before they died.

If God gave you an extra 24 hours on top of your life, or maybe just another hour, what would you do?

We are creatures of habit, spending our time much as we've always done. So the day (or hour) may look very much the same, because that's how we are, full of distractions, thoughts, wishes, feelings, just as the last 24 hours. It's us, we're human. Because that time will be so full, it will be full of us and the things we do. Whatever our lives are made up of, whatever we usually do or think about, these will occupy our dying moments on earth. It's us, it's what we do, it's how we live and die. This is how people will remember us.

For some death comes quickly, for others lingeringly painfully, still others in comas. Whatever their last moments turn out to be, for some their private dying turns into public debate in a Coroners court. What would you have them say about you, what would you change?

Paul, ever the one for suggestions, exhorts the Ephesians to change their ways: "Speak to one another with psalms, hymns and spiritual songs. Sing and make music in your heart to the Lord, always giving thanks to God the Father for everything, in the name of our Lord Jesus Christ" (Ephesians 5:19-20). Not sure if we're all up for that all the time, even in our last 24 hours – well possibly just a bit.

One question still remains: if this really is my last hour, the very last one, was my life a life well spent, did I make a difference, even just a tiny one?

Change yourself, change the world. Peter did (John 21:15).

Prayer

Lord if this is my last hour, the very last one on earth, help me to feel your presence close to me, guide me through my last 60 minutes, show me how you would have me live my last hour. Thank you for my life Lord, the gifts you have given me, and help me use my life here on earth. Amen.

Memory verse

Matthew 5:13

"You are the salt of the earth, but if the salt loses its saltiness, how can it be made salty again? It is no longer good for anything, except to be thrown out and trampled by men."

Action

Think about the last 24 hours. What did you do? What did you like or dislike? Now add to those images one person you kind of know, who might benefit from an invite to tea this afternoon. Even if they say no thanks, at least you've asked them. Maybe ask someone else for tea?

Day 20

Love me ... as this is all there is

Reading: 1 Corinthians 13:4-7

⁴ Love is patient, love is kind. It does not envy, it does not boast, it is not proud. ⁵ It is not rude, it is not self-seeking, it is not easily angered, it keeps no record of wrongs. ⁶ Love does not delight in evil but rejoices with the truth. ⁷ It always protects, always trusts, always hopes, always perseveres.

Meditation

Can I tell you who I am, please?

"I don't like cabbage!" bawled the girl at her Mum. Mum puts on her 'I'm going to tell you' face and replies "Neither do I so eat them up."

We don't have to like everything or everyone, but saying so is very hard. Social expectations or just good manners require we should at least try a little, leaving the rest on the side of the plate. Humbug! Why should I? It's awful, especially if it's over cooked – yuck!

So much for cabbage – what about our friendships, which on occasions are not too dissimilar from overcooked cabbage, having bits we don't exactly like? We too come with bits we don't like or won't even talk about, and then there's the bits we wish would drop off. Some we can change; hair colour, body shape, eyes, or noses. Even attractiveness comes bottle shaped, but we don't. We also come with history, our personal CV, our experiences of living that have brought us to now, the baggage we've acquired, or in some instances had imposed upon us, our physical attributes that we can't hide (unless I diet or use hair dye!), as well as our personalities that always leak out, no matter how carefully we try concealing them, no matter what concealer we use!

With these comes another part: the bits of us we're scared or frightened of, our regrets, the 'me' that I won't even go near because I'm too ashamed, it's too painful, too sad, too embarrassing. I may be so ashamed of some parts of my life that there is no way you would ever understand, never. If I told you, you would go. You would never love me, not really love me, ever again, ever! I did say ever again didn't I?

Our wounded secrets, our pain, our hurt or sadness lingers inside, available to no one else but us, blocking our potential and holding us back. No matter how many times we say we're sorry, memories linger, squashing potential and hurting ambition. What if they knew? How would they react? We've said we're so sorry. We wish we'd never done that. What if I tell you who I am? What if you walk away? What am I to do then? What if you don't like me? I wish to be known and loved for me, not my pretension. Please share and know me as I know myself.

Records don't show Jesus as succinctly saying, "I am who I am; love me or not." He is recorded as asking his disciples, "Who do you say I am?" (Mark 8:29). Peter replies, "You are the Christ." Peter could only have answered if he knew Jesus well. Jesus' question shows how we too, if we trust someone enough, can ask them for an honest opinion and let them tell us what they see of our behaviour and pattern of life.

For Jesus, letting others know Him, and getting to know them was important. Knowing and being known is, unfortunately, not an overnight event. The Psalmist puts it like this, "O LORD, you have searched me and you know me. You know when I sit and when I rise; you perceive my thoughts from afar. You discern my going out and my lying down; you are familiar with all my ways. Before a word is on my tongue you know it completely, O LORD" (Psalm 135:1-4). Mmm, quite a bit of knowing going on – lots of trust with personal information and feelings. In order to be able to share we need to know ourselves. If asked the question, "Tell me something about yourself," how many would reply with facts and a splattering of emotions? It's easier to share information about ourselves than our emotional attachments to that information. We hide behind our information mask, all protected and comfy, never letting the real us out for others to see, for them to love.

To love me I need to tell you about me, not all in one go, but just the bits I can manage to share. Letting someone know us comes with a risk they'll dislike what they find. Our human nature is one of often rejecting the unpleasant, frowning when someone tells us what they've really done. There is however little new here. Our modern lifestyles are full of anxious feelings, missed opportunities, wrongs we've done or have had done to us. 300 years before Jesus was born we find the Psalmists wailing about their fears and failures. 2300 years later not much has changed. Nothing's really new. God has seen it all before. Only today we call it something new and terrifying, because it still is. Sharing ourselves with those around us is still, and will remain, a painful experience for some.

What if I tell you all about me? There will be nothing else to tell. What if you still don't like me? What then?

Jesus speaks of comfort from His own Father, such as only as a father could comfort, comfort which is freely offered to everyone with no strings, no conditions. As Jesus' Father loves him, He too loves us. John puts it like this: "...let the world know that you sent me and have loved them even as you have loved me" (John 17:23). And earlier at 14:21: "Whoever has my commands and obeys them, he is the one who loves me. He who loves me will be loved by my Father, and I too will love him and show myself to him." We are never just alone, no matter how hard we try, no matter where we flee, or what we hide under, or flee to. In the darkest place we can imagine there is a person waiting for us, Jesus.

And next, next is wherever or to whoever Jesus leads us. In the first instance it may be ourselves, reviewing our lives, being honest with ourselves, taking a step of being known by others. Or it may be to others, doing what Jesus advised a young lawyer: "Love your neighbour as yourself" (Luke 10:27). Love is never far from Jesus' lips.

On the whole we tend to look out for ourselves. We might not always like what we find, sometimes screaming that we don't like cabbage on our plate. Whether it's our cabbage or someone else's, Jesus asks us, "Can you love them? I do, will you?"

Prayer

Father help me understand how I feel, and help me to share my feelings with others. Let me be responsive and loving when someone shares with me how they feel. Give me the words or silence when I am with them. Father I pray for our world of pain and suffering. Help me to be instrumental in caring for the hurt in our world.

Memory verse

John 16:33

"I have told you these things, so that in me you may have peace. In this world you will have trouble. But take heart! I have overcome the world."

Action

What's your favourite time of day to sit and relax? What's your favourite way of relaxing? Go and tell someone else about how you relax, and ask them how they relax. At the same time ask if they would like to chat about anything that's on their mind.

Day 21

Just who controls me then?

Reading: Matthew 6:24

²⁴ "No one can serve two masters. Either he will hate the one and love the other, or he will be devoted to the one and despise the other. You cannot serve both God and Money."

Meditation

What is it about two masters? Can't I job share? When it comes to God and money, Jesus teaches no, even with a heavily worded contract. Why is this? Money looks so innocent and secure – nothing to fear. But money comes with a health warning: 'BEWARE'.

Juggling two masters comes with 'horns of a dilemma'. How do I decide, and can I change my mind later? Following God's design for our life requires obedience, faith, and reliance on God; but money is good – we still need it, or do the shops barter now?

Money and God form integral parts of our lives. Understanding these necessitates stepping outside ourselves into the mind of a Gospel writer such as Matthew. He wrote, 'Οὐδεὶς δύναται δυσὶ κυρίοις δουλεύειν, …' (Matthew 6:24), which in the NIV comes out as, 'No one can serve two masters…' From the words, 'κυρίοις δουλεύειν' we get, 'serve master'. 'κύριος' gives us 'belonging to someone' or 'subject to someone who decides'. 'δουλεύω' is being a slave, being owned, yielding obedience, or giving up yourself. A longer translation might be: 'No one through their own ability can belong, or be slave to, two owners'. Being 'owned' is very different from being a servant or 'subject to a master'.

A master gives you time off. A slave owner holds your life in their hands. They have total ownership. You have no rights, no time off. As a slave you stopped being a person, you were an object of value. Matthew equates slavery with money's influence over us. He asks a stinging question: does money own us? In some instances he rather thinks it may.

England no longer has slavery. It ended with the Slavery Abolition Act 1833. Curiously though, compensation was paid, not to the slaves but to their owners. Over £20 million (1833 value) was paid to former slave owners for freeing their slaves. A single slave was valued at around £19.00 (1833 prices). Slaves were a commodity, bought as tools for work or entertainment. Instead of giving compensation to the former slave, it went to the owner. They were bought out of slavery at a price. This is the point Matthew is making: being a slave of someone or something removes your rights. You are no longer you – you are controlled by your owner. If that owner is money, then you are its commodity. This is the level of slavery Matthew speaks of, the one with a health warning. If I allow myself to think of money as my primary goal in life, then I abdicate my rights and I am its slave.

There is another side (remember the dilemma horns). It's also about how we 'use' money and decide on our level of reliance upon it. As the writer of Timothy says about it, money comes with a health warning, not a prohibition.

In 1 Timothy 6:10 we read that the love of money is a root of all kinds of evil. Money, possessions or wealth itself is not the problem. It's our attitude and our use of it. Here, we may become enslaved by it, because of an attitude change. Money is not actually the problem – we are. The problem is how we think about money, placing our trust in it to keep us going.

It's all to do with who we trust. If I trust God, I know that because God cares and loves me, He will look out for me. If I trust money, then I need a good accountant and a lot of financial insight. If I feel I need to trust, then I either need more money or I need more God. It all depends on where I place my trust.

God gives exceptional interest rates, very good returns, and no charges. Trust though is a two way street. If I trust God, God also will trust me, trusting me with money and possessions. (I suspect it's God who trusts first). To see this trust in action, here are some questions.

How much do we care about what enslaves us?
Look around the room you're sitting in. What is the most precious thing that you can find? Now think of giving it up if your partner's life depended upon it. But would you give it up if you had the option to pay it off in instalments. Would you give it away? What if fire broke out? What would you first take out of your house? (The answer is the fire! but after that?) Or consider this, the marauding hoards intent on destroying you and your possessions will be here in 10 minutes. What do you take with you?

How do I use the things I've been entrusted with?
The things sitting on my shelf: do they just sit and stare back? Would I let someone borrow one? What if they said yes? How would I feel once they'd borrowed it? Would I wonder how they were using it? Would I want it back there and then? How would I cope if they broke it?

How much do I trust God?
Do I see myself as reliant upon Him for all my needs? Do I see myself as reliant upon Him for any of my needs, for just a few, or for none of them? Am I reliant upon God to affirm that I need him? Am I reliant upon Him to be there when I choose to need him?

Is love the most important part of our lives?
Without love, I am the rushing wind on route to nowhere? With love, I am the one who cares. Do we care?

Love is just one point of a triangle. Another is who my Master is. The last one is Jesus, as Saviour. Triangles stand for many things. Here as a symbol of who controls our life. Without God at the centre, our billowing lives may rush directionless, enslaved by what we hold dear.

Prayer

Father, show me what's precious in my life and where my trust really rests. Show me how to use what you've given me, for you. Help me not be engulfed by the commercialism this world entertains, but show me where your resources can be used in my life to effect change around me. Help me where I am materially minded, to see this is how my life is run. Help me to see, and to think what I want to do about it. Amen.

Memory verse

Matthew 6:24

"No one can serve two Masters. Either he will hate the one and love the other, or he will be devoted to the one and despise the other. You cannot serve both God and Money."

Action

Let someone borrow something which you hold dear, but you seriously would not mind if it got broken or damaged.

Day 22

How to love others from where you are

Reading: John 19:25-27

²⁵ Near the cross of Jesus stood his mother, his mother's sister, Mary the wife of Clopas, and Mary Magdalene. ²⁶ When Jesus saw his mother there, and the disciple whom he loved standing nearby, he said to his mother, "Dear woman, here is your son," ²⁷ and to the disciple, "Here is your mother." From that time on, this disciple took her into his home.

Meditation

Love only complicates matters. It gets in the way. It's too precious to share with anyone. If you do, they only hurt you. Love never solves any problems, often making them worse. Love is outdated in our modern world. Love will not survive in our secularised society. Love was such a 1960's thing, today we know better. Love is all about me. I have to love myself to be happy; no one else will, right?

Thankfully, that's not the view of everyone. But imagine it is your view. What if your life was based on these principles, where would your comfort come from? Who do you turn to when it gets rough? Who loves you enough to care about what happens to you?

So where are we on the 'who loves me' front?

Love Audit

Paper and Pencil required – there are some spare pages at the back of the book.

- Who defines what love is? Or, more appropriately, who do we let define what love is in our lives?

- How loving am I being to my family and friends, people around me?

- How is my life as a loving person different from my life a month ago? Two months ago? Last year? What has changed inside me, if anything, and what or whom might have affected me?

Take your paper and pencil and see what you come up with.

Who defines love in our lives?

Jesus says His Father is the source of all life, of everything, so He must also be the source of all love. God himself confirms He's a God of love: "Then a cloud appeared and enveloped them, and a voice came from the cloud: This is my Son, whom I love. Listen to him!" (Mark 9:7). Jesus puts his Father's gift of love into action when He says of the growing church and people, they are to … ove each other (John 15:17). This is an active love, not one waiting for the other person to have a need. We are to love the world; but with a caveat. Paul, speaking about love, clarifies *how* we are to love: "Love must be sincere. Hate what is evil. Cling to what is good" (Romans 12:9).

Alternatively, we can take love from what the world offers. Except our world does not always want what's best for us, too frequently wanting what's in its best interests, not ours. It's a world of take, not give, of looking the part at the expense of others. Luke, often blunt and to the point, puts it like this: "If you love those who love you, what credit is that to you? Even 'sinners' love those who love them" (Luke 6:32). Are we then to act differently in how we apply love to the world?

Writing to the Galatians about love and God's law, Paul comments: "The entire law is summed up in a single command: Love your neighbour as yourself" (Galatians 5:14). But I don't always love me. In fact, I'm often frustrated at what I do. I don't like me, I get annoyed with myself, I hurt like there's no tomorrow, I feel the world owes me so much, I want and no one comes to me. Is this the type of love Paul speaks of? For some it may be. Paul writes further: "Love does no harm to its neighbour. Therefore love is the fulfilment of the law" (Romans 13:10). Hang on, if I am to, "…do no harm…" to my neighbour, and also love my neighbour as myself, I should be loving myself and my neighbour to the same level. But that's hard, as I'm not too good at loving me, not always, not all the time.

How loving am I being to my family, my friends, people around me?

Jesus' example above shows love at the sharp end. Jesus knew He was going to die, even though He was to rise from the dead three days later. He knew His mum would miss Him, and He needed her to be cared for. Enter the disciple whom Jesus loved. On the cross Jesus is resolving a domestic matter. A single woman (at this point in time Joseph had died) would have found it difficult to provide for herself. The loved disciple was the answer: another family unit created. Each could care for the other as their needs arose.

How is my life as a loving person different from my life as a loving person a month ago? Two months ago? Last year? What, if anything, has changed me?

We change, not because we grow older, but through the influence the Holy Spirit has on how we live as we grow older. A young person can be filled with such passion and love for God, more than someone of greater years, as age is not a determinant of God's presence in our lives. More maybe expected of older generations, but not so with God. He calls each one of us to be part of his family, with responsibilities in that family, irrespective of our age or experience. Your responsibilities might be obvious, or it may take you years to discover them. If in doubt, God is very good at helping us in our search.

Families are important to Jesus. Each one of us has a family. We may not like or love them, any or all of the time, but we have them. Families are intrinsic to Jesus ministry. At the centre of His ministry is the creation of a new family, us with Him. This is Jesus' own wider family. When Jesus was walking the earth, the Jewish community rejected Him. It was said of Jesus that He, "... came to that which was His own, but His own did not receive Him" (John 1:11). Jesus, whilst dying on the cross, creates a new family. Knowing He will soon be leaving earth and returning to His Father, He knows He needs to provide for those He loves. Here He demonstrates our own necessity to create families for those around us, to live with and to be loved.

Our love audit will change over time, just as our relationships inside and outside our families change. Where families are torn apart through events, lies or physical destruction, Jesus points us to His own circumstances, and asks these questions: Who is in your family? Where are they now? Do you need to form another one, or enlarge the one you have with someone who needs caring for?

On the cross, Jesus joined together His mum and the disciple He loved as a new family. Who can you think of who might like to join your family?

Prayer

Lord, show me who you would include in my family. Help me to see their needs, and show me how I can make a difference. Lord, teach me to love and understand my own family. Heal our differences and open us to be more caring for each other. Amen.

Memory verse

Matthew 5:46

If you love those who love you, what reward will you get? Are not even the tax collectors doing that?

Action

Is there someone you know whose family live a little distance from them, or someone who does not have a family as such? Invite them to come for a meal and a chat. Alternatively, is there someone at a distance who would value you friendship via post, email, or text?

If you're not in a family and would like to be, or your family live a distance away, have a chat at your local place of worship about linking up with someone, or join a home group for some support, even if just for a short time.

Day 23

How to love others by listening to them

Reading: 1 Corinthians 13:9-12

[9] For we know in part and we prophesy in part, [10] but when perfection comes, the imperfect disappears. [11] When I was a child, I talked like a child, I thought like a child, I reasoned like a child. When I became a man, I put childish ways behind me. [12] Now we see but a poor reflection as in a mirror; then we shall see face to face. Now I know in part; then I shall know fully, even as I am fully known.

Meditation

Is listening all it's cracked up to be? We can listen to some people for hours. Others we're craving to go in minutes. It sometimes depends on who they are and what they're saying, but more importantly it depends on our interest in them and what they're saying – our attraction to them. The more we're interested in someone, the more reasons we'll stop and listen. Likewise with what they're saying: even if it's dull and boring we'll still stay and listen, if we're attracted to them. This attraction is not necessarily romantic, and in most cases it's quite the opposite. We're interested because who they are and/or what they're saying sparks off in us a connection to them.

People tend to talk for several reasons. These include: a) I want to share with you myself and my views so you can understand me better; b)

I just have to tell you, otherwise I'm going to explode, even if you don't want to listen to me; or c) listen to me – I'm talking, not you.

So listening can sometimes be a three way conversation: you, me (and me again). Conversations may also consist of germane information with ancillary words – almost background noise to what the person really wants to say.

For many people, listening or attending to others is not easy, as it involves just that: stopping and listening. It means no thinking up those witty repartees, no contemplating or cognitively wandering off about what they're saying, no jumping in or interrupting with our own questions or thoughts, and certainly no walking away. It's just sitting patiently, waiting, and listening. Once they've stopped, please do all of the above, but only once they've stopped talking. Listening is staying our minds to focus on the speaker, their words, tone, manner of speech, phrasing, non-verbal signs and behaviour. It's listening and watching them before we start thinking about what we want to say back. And if I don't listen, what's the result? A multiplicity of missed opportunities, poor social interactions, ignored advice, and failed relationships. We miss so much of those around us by not actually listening to them properly, as King David found out.

David, one of the great Jewish rulers, found if he didn't listen to God he kept getting it wrong. In 2 Samuel 12 Nathan tells David how his sin is upsetting God. Psalm 51 records David, who was sunk in despair, recognising his fault and crying out to God, seeking comfort and reconciliation. We're not all fortunate to have a Nathan, but we can follow his example of listening to those around us. Nathan stands up to David, a powerful king, rebuking his actions. Telling someone they are wrong is no easy task, particularly someone of David's standing (David had just had Uriah the Hittite killed). Listening, as David found, is very hard.

Jesus was acutely aware of listening and its power. He had lots of practice with the Jewish leaders of the time, in their attempts at trapping Him into saying what they wanted to hear, so that they could get rid of Him. Jesus listened very carefully, catching the questioners out with their own questions. Only when He was ready did He let them kill Him.

Jesus regards listening as pivotal in our relationships. He commanded his disciples what to do if people didn't listen to them: "If anyone will not welcome you or listen to your words, shake the dust off your feet when you leave that home or town" (Matthew 10: 14). How many times have we said, "If only I'd listened," but we don't, with resulting consequences and dust everywhere.

And if we fail to listen or text back, what's the other person's experience of us? It's frequently one of upset, and occasionally anger and resentment we're not paying attention to them. Jesus was acutely aware of being ignored, of being alone, alone in the silence. In the Garden of Gethsemane He cries out to His Father to take away the cup of suffering. (This is the cup described in Jeremiah 25:15, the cup of God's wrath: "Take from my hand this cup filled with the wine of my wrath and make all the nations to whom I send you drink it.") Jesus at this point seeks another way for God to carry out His mission; but we see God turning His back on His only Son. The way is set; there is no other way to redeem mankind. The Gospel writers record Jesus crying out time and time again. For Jesus, God had turned away, He was not listening.

When we do listening there is a joy in responding, in hearing words and seeing someone's face beam as we accept and understand what they've said. Matthew 21:15-16: "But when the chief priests and the teachers of the law saw the wonderful things he did and the children shouting in the temple area, 'Hosanna to the Son of David,' they were indignant. 'Do you hear what these children are saying?' they asked him. 'Yes,' replied Jesus, 'have you never read, "From the lips of children and infants you have ordained praise"?'" God as our Father longs to hear someone, who perhaps has not listened before, or has stopped listening, say, "Lord forgive me." Heaven's response is one of pure joy: "I tell you that in the same way there will be more rejoicing in heaven over one sinner who repents than over ninety-nine righteous persons who do not need to repent" (Luke 15:7).

Listening or being listened to is important to Jesus. So much so that He commands us to be listeners too. One of Jesus' most frequent words was, 'listen'. He uses it to start most crowd lectures or seminars off with: Ἀκούσατέ or listen. "Again Jesus called the crowd to him and said, 'Listen to me, everyone, and understand this'" (Mark 7:14). Listen is perhaps not the best translation. It's more 'attend to' which is closer to the original Greek. When we 'attend to' something we're no longer passive but we've become quite active about it, as listening should be.

For some of our friends, if we don't text back quick enough, we get another text asking if we're still listening, or are we asleep and gone to bed. For others the silence is painful, the ones so often ignored, forgotten, left to the silence, passed by as relief is handed out, too afraid to say "I'm here," because no one listened before. What of them? Jesus knows. He too was ignored, as His own Father turned away (Matthew 26:39).

Jesus asks of us to listen, to 'attend to' them as He did. We see Him walking the earth consoling lost and troubled people, helping those who suffer, comforting the bereaved, talking with the person sitting by the wall who's been watching the social crowd, invited but so alone. Jesus is listening and then responding. It is only through attending to their words that Jesus knows how He can attend to their physical needs.

Around us live our friends, relatives, and neighbours, who perhaps like King David, are desperately trying to rid themselves of loneliness. Isolated and longing for a chat about where they are today, with today's struggles, let alone the ones of tomorrow. Sometimes there is nothing we can say – only be there, holding their hand, if that's what they need.

We don't have to say anything, just listen to them. Could we listen enough to show we care?

Prayer

Lord, help me to stop talking when I should be listening. Help me to hear what is not being said. Help me to attend to the needs of my friends and family. Father, forgive me where I have jumped in with unfitting words before they have finished speaking. Help me to wait and be your listening servant to those around me. Amen.

Memory verse

Proverbs 18:13

He who answers before listening – that is his folly and his shame.

Action

Spend some time today listening to your friends, family, next door neighbours, or the person at the next desk. Before you respond to them, wait a few seconds, and then say whatever it is. Make sure you are listening, really listening, not waiting for them to stop so that you can say your piece.

Day 24

How to love others - love in a fallen world

Reading: Ecclesiastes 9:1-4

¹ So I reflected on all this and concluded that the righteous and the wise and what they do are in God's hands, but no man knows whether love or hate awaits him. ² All share a common destiny – the righteous and the wicked, the good and the bad, the clean and the unclean, those who offer sacrifices and those who do not.

> As it is with the good man,
>   so with the sinner;
> as it is with those who take oaths,
>   so with those who are afraid to take them.

³ This is the evil in everything that happens under the sun: The same destiny overtakes all. The hearts of men, moreover, are full of evil and there is madness in their hearts while they live, and afterward they join the dead. ⁴ Anyone who is among the living has hope – even a live dog is better off than a dead lion!

Meditation

At the end of life, standing in front of God, with God asking the questions, will you be able to say "I loved a fallen world," even a tiny bit?

Ecclesiastes speaks of life's experiences and of our world's bizarre twists and turns, where a life not centred on God becomes fruitless and meaningless. "Mmmmmmm" and maybe "humbug" we might say; are these not the ramblings of an old man? Theologians speculate the writer is Solomon (the King and famous baby divider). If so, what brought him to write such painful laments? Whoever the writer, what is clear he's deeply dissatisfied with his life – it's unfulfilled and full of regrets. If, one day, you do find yourself standing before God, feeling regretful of your life, if you do, you will have at least one friend, the writer of Ecclesiastes.

Of all the Old Testament books, Ecclesiastes provides perhaps the most succinct of warnings. If you don't have God at your centre, this is what you get, take it or leave it. Not a happy thought, and perhaps with a reason. The writer speaks of toil and of wisdom, the centres of many of our lives, as meaningless, only bringing sorrow and grief (Ecclesiastes 1:18). We may well ask "Why bother?!"

It is however life's pleasures which cause greater concern. In Ecclesiastes 2:3 we read, "I tried cheering myself with wine..." (v.4), "I undertook great projects..." (v.8), "I amassed silver and gold for myself..." (v.10), "I denied myself nothing my eyes desired, I refused my heart no pleasure..." Despite enjoying the world's pleasures, this left him unsatisfied. The penultimate verse of chapter 12 provides the answer: "Fear God and keep His commandments; for this is the whole duty of man" (Ecclesiastes 12:13). It is with pity then we need to consider the writers life. Only right at the end finally working it out: "Oh, I see it now. If I have God as the centre of my being it all makes sense. Why did no one say, please tell me why, surely you knew?"

On his way through life he seems to have discovered some hints at where true happiness may be found. For example, he says in chapter 3:1, "There is a time for everything, and a season for every activity under heaven." There is a time to be born, to die, to weep and mourn, to search and keep, to be silent, and to love.

Throughout his laments, laments of a seemingly wasted life, there comes a sense of actual purpose, of discovery. The writer spends so much time moaning about how his life is working out (or rather not) that his discovery of God could easily be missed. He seems almost blind to it. God is there as the constant in a world of meaningless. He does not go away – we just omit to see Him. In such failure or frustration, as our lives may often seem, we only see the world as dying embers in the fire. This is all there is, nothing more. Such is our choice.

The other choice is one of seeing God as life, life to the full, but not always as we expect or want it. We just need to open our eyes and consider, as the writer does: "This is …what God has done…" (Ecclesiastes 7:13) and, "Then I saw all that God had done. No one can comprehend what goes on under the sun. Despite all his efforts to search it out, man cannot discover its meaning. We are all a mixture of good and evil" (Ecclesiastes 8:17, 9:1). And here's the difference: one person sees themselves as they are, the fool does not. It does not matter if we take a lifetime to realise this, only that we do eventually realise it. We may have missed out on so much of God's presence and love in our lives (which itself is painful); but we've got there in the end. The fool, alas, has not.

How we use this recognition is fostered by this new found gift of God in our lives.

Take another look at Ecclesiastes. This time, try and see our lives as God sees them, lives of opportunities, of love for others, of nothing ever being wasted, even if we cannot see how it works out. There is never a wasted life or moment with God.

We often recognise things in our lives through seeing opposites. If we are unloved then we know what the feeling is, if we become loved the feelings change; an opposite is created. Read Ecclesiastes, replacing meaningless with its opposite, and adding God in what's being said. It then comes alive. For instance, "'Meaningless! Meaningless!' says the Teacher, 'Utterly meaningless! Everything is meaningless'" (Ecclesiastes

1:2), becomes "'Meaningful! Meaningful!' says the Teacher, 'Utterly meaningful! Everything is meaningful'" All we have done is add God into the equation.

Without God the writer of Ecclesiastes is correct – the world is meaningless. With God, the perspective changes, and we come to see things as God sees them, and then it makes more sense. If we see our world as one of meaning, with God as the source of that meaning, should we not also be sharing this discovery with others. If not, then they will continue living in a world which is meaningless, because they do not have God. They will continue to miss out on the love God can give them, a love from God their Father in a world of meaninglessness and fear.

The concept of love is complex in Ecclesiastes because of the negativity of the writer, who struggles with his seemingly wasted years: "A time to love and a time to hate, a time for war and a time for peace" (Ecclesiastes 3:8). With God, nothing is ever wasted. All has a use, even if we can't see this at the time. Often we can't see it because we are part of what is happening at the time. Once we get to the end of life, then we see things more clearly, seeing Jesus as the opposite of everything Ecclesiastes represents. In 1 Corinthians 13:8-10, Paul says of love and life, "Love never fails. But where there are prophecies, they will cease; where there are tongues, they will be stilled; where there is knowledge, it will pass away. For we know in part and we prophesy in part, but when perfection comes, the imperfect disappears."

The writer concludes in Ecclesiastes 9:1 reflecting on his life: "So I reflected on all this and concluded that the righteous and the wise and what they do are in God's hands, but no man knows whether love or hate awaits him." Except we do, as 1 Corinthians 13:13 points out: "And now these three remain: faith, hope and love. But the greatest of these is love."

Ecclesiastes will always be a book of moans, because the moaner does not recognise the need for God till the end of his life. He also did not have Jesus as the love that overcomes all the moaning in the world. Who do you fancy being: a moaner or a lover to those around you?

Only through the love we receive from God can we share a love for a fallen world.

Prayer

Father, thank you for your love in my life, for the comfort you give me when all seems wasted and fruitless, when the world is too much for me and I want to leave. Father, help me to see that you are there as the constant of my life, no matter what's happened, and that no matter where I've been or what I've done, nothing is ever wasted. Thank you that you have such a purpose for my life. Help me see where you would have me serve you now.

Memory verse

Ecclesiastes 12:13

Now all has been heard; here is the conclusion of the matter: Fear God and keep his commandments, for this is the whole duty of man.

Action

Do you know someone (and this might be you too) who tends to see things more often from the negative end of the stick than from the other end. Our life, as Ecclesiastes paints, is often full of sticky stick ends. Today, go and find someone whose life is at the sticky end of the stick, and chat to them about the opposites that Ecclesiastes talks about.

Day 25

How to love others - living for Jesus

Readings

Philippians 1:7-8

⁷ It is right for me to feel this way about all of you, since I have you in my heart; for whether I am in chains or defending and confirming the gospel, all of you share in God's grace with me. ⁸ God can testify how I long for all of you with the affection of Christ Jesus.

1 Thessalonians 1:2-5

² We always thank God for all of you, mentioning you in our prayers. ³ We continually remember before our God and Father your work produced by faith, your labour prompted by love, and your endurance inspired by hope in our Lord Jesus Christ. ⁴ For we know, brothers loved by God, that he has chosen you, ⁵ because our gospel came to you not simply with words, but also with power, with the Holy Spirit and with deep conviction. You know how we lived among you for your sake.

Meditation

There are no part-time Christians. There may be Christians who only think and pray to God every so often, but they are still Christians. The Gospels don't record Jesus only being partially crucified for us. Paul was not put in chains because he preached a risen Jesus on the weekends, and did a bit of tent making during the week. Although there's lots of part time Christian work, there are only full-time Christians, just as there are no part-time friends. It's quite hard to be a part-time friend. Try it. The more times we say to someone, "Sorry, I'm busy, I can't see you today," the more we lose touch with them, and the more our friendship starts to wain. They may remain our friend, but we have moved away. Jesus says of our relationship with Him: you are either for me or against me. There's no half way ground, which means that there are no half-way Christians. Either you're for Jesus or you're not.

Equally, there is no part time poverty. An individual's poverty exists 24/7. There are no weekend breaks for them. The Saturday food shopping list still remains very small, no matter where you shop, as there is little money for food. The monthly clothes bill and days out with the family are often non-existent, as no one has enough money to spare. "It's quite hard to be poor part-time, as no one understands I'd like to share just a little of your money. All they see is me asking for money, not the home I do not have, or the food I'll never eat." The poor have become the no ones we all see every day, the 'no ones in particular'. We walk past them with our full-time friends, on the way to our full-time day out with fully paid for fun. Poverty fails to recognise social class or what we once were. It strikes with its pain and hardship, irrespective of what a person's life was. Either you're rich or poor. There is no half way measure, no part-time poverty, no time off. To this poverty came Jesus, to serve and show His followers His mission to the world.

Biblical records show Jesus initially calling twelve people to follow Him, as well as numerous others who joined Him as His ministry unfolded. Perhaps not all of this larger group were privy to the intimate conversations as the first twelve were, but they were there too, hearing what He said, seeing His ministry develop. We hear about the disciples' triumphs, their squabbles and secrets, how they failed to 'get what Jesus was going on about this time!' In there, amongst the disciples, we may see ourselves on our own journey to understand Jesus, trying like them to work out what this Jesus is all about.

The Biblical Jesus may sometimes seem a bit too nice, too written like a story. We forget the arguments with authorities, the off road journeys across Galilee, or nights camped out with only what you're wearing. We may occasionally imagine Jesus in a green field having lunch, running a small group session with some of the disciples, or praying quietly before settling down to chat over a drink. We may see His disciples trying to remember what He's said, so the Gospels can get written or sailing around in boats on the Galilean sea; a cinematic Jesus, but still a Jesus who changes the world. There was no part-time Jesus. He was God all the time with a full-time mission, a mission He'd like us to join too, if we choose. He's not necessarily asking we take to the dusty roads, or camp out over night, but He is saying "Follow me, do as I do." Jesus knows being a full-time Christian is hard. It is full of decisions over money and time, and saying no to pleasures which today's world counts as normal.

The first disciples followed Jesus knowing very little about His expectations of them. Today we follow Jesus in almost the same position. We don't know where our walk with God will take us. We don't know what He will ask us to do for Him. In all of this there is Jesus saying, "I will not leave you abandoned. Here is the Holy Spirit to fill you with power and energy to keep you going."

When we say to Jesus, "Yes please, come into my life," we are filled with the Holy Spirit, and our lives are transformed, we become lights shining in this dark world. Most of us, at one time or another, will feel very little. There may also be times when we feel that God has left us – times when we feel we're lightless. John talks of, "Our light shining in the world," and later on, "The light shines in the darkness, but the darkness has not understood it" (John1:5). We are that light, shinning in the darkness with the power of the Holy Spirit inside us, lighting us up. We are not appearing dimly, but we are glowing in the dark. There may be times when we need a bit more of God in our lives to carry us through the difficult patches, but God still shines in us. Without His light, we live in darkness. There are no part-time lights. Either they're on or off. They may be on a dimmer switch so you can turn them down a bit, but they are still either on or off. You can't be a part-time Christian. If you could, Jesus would have said so.

God recognises deeply our human frailty (He tried it once when He lived amongst us); He also understands how our old life, the one before we knew Jesus, keeps ebbing back into us, trying to stop us living for Him. The Holy Spirit supports us in our battle with this, encouraging us to change our behaviour. He also asks us to pray, talking daily with Him about what's going on in us, which unfortunately for some is a hard daily challenge.

We are not alone in finding being a full-time Christian hard work. The church in Thessalonica was also having difficulties in this respect, which prompted Paul to write to them. He said they should follow the pattern set by Jesus: prayerfulness, obedience, Godliness, self denial, and love. We may struggle with these some of the time, but Jesus knows we're not perfect. This also is part of being a shining light. If you look at a candle, there's always those little bits on the side, which don't look too nice, the bits which could never contribute the flame, yet they do, helping the candle burn brightly. With God in our life, the 'all of us' can be used, even the bits where we've gone a bit wrong, because that is part of being human. This is the light shinning in the darkness which the darkness cannot understand. It's how God uses our frail humanity to bring about His kingdom. It doesn't make sense, but then no one said God had to.

Prayer

Father, there are often times when I do not understand you or your ways, where you are leading, or how on earth I'm going to get there. Be with me and fill me with Your Holy Spirit. Help me shine, even when my shininess is lacking. Show me Lord where you would like me to be a full-time Christian for you and show me the work you have in mind for me. Amen.

Memory verse

Matthew 8:20

Jesus replied, "Foxes have holes and birds of the air have nests, but the Son of Man has no place to lay his head."

Action

Is there someone you know, or have read about, who may need a bit of financial help today?

Day 26

How to love others - receiving love

Reading: Luke 15:11-32

When you read the passage, don't look for who's right, but for who's trying to make the best of a bad situation...

The Parable of the Lost Son

[11] Jesus continued: "There was a man who had two sons. [12] The younger one said to his father, 'Father, give me my share of the estate.' So he divided his property between them. [13] Not long after that, the younger son got together all he had, set off for a distant country and there squandered his wealth in wild living. [14] After he had spent everything, there was a severe famine in that whole country, and he began to be in need. [15] So he went and hired himself out to a citizen of that country, who sent him to his fields to feed pigs. [16] He longed to fill his stomach with the pods that the pigs were eating, but no one gave him anything. [17] When he came to his senses, he said, 'How many of my father's hired men have food to spare, and here I am starving to death! [18] I will set out and go back to my father and say to him: 'Father, I have sinned against heaven and against you. [19] I am no longer worthy to be called your son; make me like one of your hired men.' [20] So he got up and went to his father. But while he was still a long way off, his father saw him and was filled with compassion for him; he ran to his son, threw his arms around him and kissed him. [21] The son said to him, 'Father, I have sinned against heaven and against you. I am no longer worthy to be called your son.' [22] But the father said to his servants, 'Quick! Bring the best robe and put it on him. Put a ring on his finger and sandals on his feet. [23] Bring the fattened calf

and kill it. Let's have a feast and celebrate. ²⁴ For this son of mine was dead and is alive again; he was lost and is found.' So they began to celebrate. ²⁵ Meanwhile, the older son was in the field. When he came near the house, he heard music and dancing. ²⁶ So he called one of the servants and asked him what was going on. ²⁷ 'Your brother has come,' he replied, 'and your father has killed the fattened calf because he has him back safe and sound.' ²⁸ The older brother became angry and refused to go in. So his father went out and pleaded with him. ²⁹ But he answered his father, 'Look! All these years I've been slaving for you and never disobeyed your orders. Yet you never gave me even a young goat so I could celebrate with my friends. ³⁰ But when this son of yours who has squandered your property with prostitutes comes home, you kill the fattened calf for him!' ³¹ 'My son,' the father said, 'you are always with me, and everything I have is yours. ³² But we had to celebrate and be glad, because this brother of yours was dead and is alive again; he was lost and is found.'"

Meditation

Loving someone who hurt us or ignores our advice is always rather hard. We feel perplexed at what they've done, unsure how to treat them, and certainly hesitant about trusting them. And here we have these two boys. It's always boys, never a boy and his big sister or a couple of girls. It's the boys who get into trouble!

Both boys here are equally justified in their actions, not because they're right, but for entirely divergent reasons. The errant boy sees how his life has turned out and desperately wants to change. The obedient boy compares his life with that of the errant one (what it could have been) and wants a change. Notice how 'the father' goes out to both his boys, and treats both equally, although each feels differently towards him. The father reaches out to them: to one to hear his pleas for compassion, to the other to bring compassion. Both are equally valuable to him; each certainly has differing needs, yet each responds differently to their father's love.

The second boy seems to have ignored the opportunities of love offered by his father. He may have spent all those years working for him, but the passage shows he does not know his father, not really. If he'd known what his father was like, he would have realised that he'd go out to his errant boy, welcoming him home. It almost seems as if he's wasted the life his father presented him with, to share in his love and way of life.

As the father welcomes home his errant boy, we see how love is shared, as well as how love may be received. We may offer love, but it is up to the other person to decide if they wish to receive it. Just as we can't force God upon someone, so we can't force love on them.

Jesus was quite clear about love. It is a gift from God, a central gift. Where it's squandered, it is harder for love to take root a second time, unless a person is truly sorry for what they've done, asking for forgiveness. The errant boy begs his father to forgive him, asking to be received back into his life. He wants love in his life again. The other boy just becomes angry when he sees the love his father showers on the errant boy. This waster boy turns up and wants more off his dad. The second son only sees what's going on with human eyes, not the eyes of his father. This is what he's missed out on too. Not only the love his father has for him, but the joy and forgiveness his father offers. He has spent all this time with his father and still he doesn't understand. It's not that his father doesn't equally love him. It's that the second boy's heart has not allowed his father to love him. He's kept it closed to his father's influences, closed to his father's attitude of love and care for other people. He may have lived in the same house for years on end, but none of his father's ways and habits seem to have seeped into him. He's seen how his father treats the servants and hired hands, and how much more they have left to spare. He sees the world only from his view of what he too can get, not what he can give as well.

Like the errant boy we may come to realise where our life's got to, seeing what could do with a sort out. Or perhaps we know we should come back to God and have another go. God is all about us having another go, as often as we like. All we have to do is come back and try again, as many times as we like, just asking Him to forgive us and help us again in our journey with Him. The errant boy didn't have to return. He could have stayed away, trying to sort out his life by himself without his father.

God cares for us and He hopes we in turn will care for others around us. Sometimes they won't ask for our help, and like the father in the passage we may need to ask, "What's up?" They may say no, and that's their choice, which we must respect. Other times they will come to us, and like the father in the passage we may need to meet them half way, because that's as close as they are going to come.

God is there, waiting to give us His love, the love that's been waiting for us. All we have to do is reach out and receive it. We can change ourselves from being just boys (or girls) into sons (and daughters) of a loving Father.

God cares, how can we?

Prayer

Father, help me care where care is a word not often heard. Let me care where care is not often seen. Help me to listen to their needs. Help me to show your love in a careless world to those who have more needs than me. Help me too, not to be too proud to ask for help when I'm in need. Amen.

Memory verse

Matthew 10:8

Heal the sick, raise the dead, cleanse those who have leprosy, drive out demons. Freely you have received, freely give.

Action

Who in your family (or circle of friends) do you not get on with as well as others? Or who do you feel you may have upset? Has now the time arrived to see where you both are with God's love and the care He has for both of you?

Day 27

God in a caring world

Reading: Exodus 33:7-11

The Tent of Meeting

⁷ Now Moses used to take a tent and pitch it outside the camp some distance away, calling it the "tent of meeting." Anyone inquiring of the LORD would go to the tent of meeting outside the camp. ⁸ And whenever Moses went out to the tent, all the people rose and stood at the entrances to their tents, watching Moses until he entered the tent. ⁹ As Moses went into the tent, the pillar of cloud would come down and stay at the entrance, while the LORD spoke with Moses. ¹⁰ Whenever the people saw the pillar of cloud standing at the entrance to the tent, they all stood and worshipped, each at the entrance to his tent. ¹¹ The LORD would speak to Moses face to face, as a man speaks with his friend. Then Moses would return to the camp, but his young aide Joshua son of Nun did not leave the tent.

Meditation

When I was decorating a few years ago we had 'indoor camping'. I screened off half our living room so we could live in one half, whilst I decorated the other half. One half was kept clean, the other messy. Some say it's still messy, even though I've finished decorating. In today's passage we see God also camping out; a special place set aside for God, separating the clean from the messy. For some this is where God has stayed put, inside the tent. Others are sceptical that God was even inside the tent in the first place. Still others question whether God could be contained inside a tent, unless you have an enormously sized one with extra space (remember God's going to make a new earth and new heaven so He needs a bit more space).

We need to consider this: not whether God did or did not exist, but does the tent need to be there at all? What's it doing? Was the tent hiding the truth, covering something up? Was it hiding humanities' mess from God? Was it there as a protection for us, or was God simply caring for us?

Was the tent hiding the truth? When someone wishes to disguise what's true, they frequently adopt something in place of it. This may be wishful ideas, principles, or sometimes a lie. There has to be something there, even an untruth, otherwise there would be nothing to talk about. For example, some who say that God doesn't exist replace what's known by many with something else. Atheists for instance talk about life starting with a piece of rock. OK, but we need something to kick start the rock into action – which is...? Well the answer can't be God, so think of something else. Darwin says we arrived here by chance and accident, natural selection. Natural selection means: if it works make another one – presupposing we know when we've arrived at the one that works. In 1859 Darwin wrote the Origin of Species, saying one day we'll dig up dinosaur bones connecting his theories of natural selection together. Over the last 130 years 1000's of fossils have been found (before this no one really dug them up). All of them show many varieties of plants and animals. What's missing are the prototypes or pre-versions, the ones Darwin says you get before today's plants and animals. Fossils, even extremely old ones, just look the same, showing the same characteristics. There's no gradual change in the fossils as Darwin predicted. We're obviously digging in the wrong place. The truth about God's nature can never be fully hidden, not even in a tent – it leaks out, someone will eventually notice. Only with Jesus was the world ready for a proper face-to-face conversation with God. Jesus, in His replies to the High Priest's questions, says that He has nothing to hide, He's openly spoken about God: "I said nothing in secret" (John 18:20). The tent was hiding a reality of God too wonderful for the world to comprehend at the time. God, as revealed through Jesus, couldn't remain hidden for long.

Covering up implies concealing for a purpose, occasionally malicious, frequently accidental. The moment Jesus died God's presence in the world was exposed as never before: "At that moment the curtain of the temple was torn in two from top to bottom. The earth shook and the rocks split. The tombs broke open and the bodies of many holy people who had died were raised to life. They came out of the tombs, and after Jesus' resurrection they went into the holy city and appeared to many people" (Matthew 27:51-53). There could no longer be any concealment, God is here. The tent has gone. Those who choose to deny the existence of God need to carefully consider how God chooses to reveal Himself in the world; making all discussion about God's existence fruitless. If your arguments need to be limited to does God exist, then the point is missed. The question is not does God exist, but how do I exist in a world where God is said to not exist.

What about hiding humanities mess from God? Our mess is frequently our passion for possessions, for things which give us pleasure, satisfactions without endurance, for this world's gain. Today, in the poorest parts of our planet, you will find children who share everything they have, mothers denying themselves food so their children can eat, and fathers whose work earns less than we would even consider thinking about. It is our mess. We need to consider what we're going to do about it.

For our protection? Seeing God (being in His presence) under the Old Testament regime often resulted in the 'seer' having a very short life 'seeing' God. It was through Jesus that God the Father chose to hang out with His people for 30 or so years. Not that there's anything scary about

God. It's just we wouldn't be able to cope, hence the original need for a tent.

Does God care for us? No, He loves us, which goes beyond just caring. As a loving God and as a father himself (Jesus is his Son), our needs command a special place with Him.

So why the tent? Tents divide in two. You're either inside or outside the tent, never both together. When the Israelites saw God coming as a pillar of cloud, they worshipped him outside the tent. Only Moses went inside and saw Him face to face. When Jesus died for our sins, the tent was pulled down. There is no more tent. God is freely accessible to all, or so it would seem. But not so fast with the 'Access to God'. There's another problem, one which we've created. Not only are some of us believing God doesn't exist, we're stopping others coming close to God with our actions, words, and way of life. We've opened our own tent making factory, with tents available in all shapes and sizes – tents in our minds.

Instead of God being inside the tent, we are. We can put these tents up ourselves, erecting as many of them in our lives as we like, to hide from God. God is still there, no matter how many tents we put up. And the tents come in a variety of options. Tents of deception: God does not exist, He does not love or care for us, Jesus never died. Tents leading others astray: our sins don't matter, live life as you like, who cares what you do. Tents of evil in all colours: tents of hate, desires, selfishness, misinformation, sex, drugs, alcohol abuse. Tents to hide from God – in case He sees us.

God is still there outside our tents. We only have to step outside to see Him clearly. Taking down our tents may take a little while as some are very big. God has not left us helpless in tent packing – Jesus will help us to pack them away.

Are you inside or outside the tent?

Prayer

Father, show me where I am blocking you out in my life. Break down the barriers I have created that stop more of you being in my life. Help me build up a relationship with you. Know me more, so that I can know how to serve you and your people. Father, forgive me where I am preventing others coming to you. Show me and them how we can work together for each other as brothers and sisters.

Memory verse

Proverbs 14:20

The poor are shunned even by their neighbours, but the rich have many friends.

Action

Carry out a brief audit of what's in your life that may be stopping you getting close to God. Have you put up tents that prevent Him coming into some areas of your life? Ask Jesus to help you pack them away.

Day 28

Fruits without actions

Reading: James 2:14-26

Faith and Deeds

[14] What good is it, my brothers, if a man claims to have faith but has no deeds? Can such faith save him? [15] Suppose a brother or sister is without clothes and daily food. [16] If one of you says to him, "Go, I wish you well; keep warm and well fed," but does nothing about his physical needs, what good is it? [17] In the same way, faith by itself, if it is not accompanied by action, is dead. [18] But someone will say, "You have faith; I have deeds." Show me your faith without deeds, and I will show you my faith by what I do. [19] You believe that there is one God. Good! Even the demons believe that – and shudder. [20] You foolish man, do you want evidence that faith without deeds is useless? [21] Was not our ancestor Abraham considered righteous for what he did when he offered his son Isaac on the altar? [22] You see that his faith and his actions were working together, and his faith was made complete by what he did. [23] And the scripture was fulfilled that says, "Abraham believed God, and it was credited to him as righteousness," and he was called God's friend. [24] You see that a person is justified by what he does and not by faith alone. [25] In the same way, was not even Rahab the prostitute considered righteous for what she did when she gave lodging to the spies and sent them off in a different direction? [26] As the body without the spirit is dead, so faith without deeds is dead.

Meditation

At the dark end of the year when nights are dimmest and breath just billows around us. Is it that Christmas is upon us with lights and fairy trees, magic moments, presents and friends, time to rest and enjoy the holidays? Or is it just another year's end we've managed to survive, not too badly this time, thank you very much? For many the latter's often true. It's a matter of survival. They've not had a fantastic year – perhaps giving an impression of all's well, hiding reality, or even ignoring it themselves.

Why jump to Christmas? What happened to Easter and all that chocolate? Christmas, like Easter, is full of new beginnings (alas not as much chocolate). It's a time to consider where we are and where we've been, what we'd like to change and what must change. At Christmas comes Jesus the Hope of the world, a precious gift hidden inside a little babe, crucified in our Church's calendar a few months later. New Year is nonetheless full of resolutions, carefully planned, freely boasted, equally broken. As we stepped into the New Year several months ago, what did we hope for? Has it come? Why not? What's stopping us?

Christians today face many challenges. Our country no longer boasts its Christianity – more its secularity. We are at the dark end of the year, hoping for a new beginning, a revival of faith. Around 2000 years ago James wrote to the 'scattered nations' about the difficulties facing them, difficulties which equally face us today. He wrote of how faith will be challenged and tested, reminding his readers of their duty to be active members of Christ's body, His church.

Week by week, today's congregations listen to the exhortations of their speakers, encouraging them in their Christian lives. Like James, they show them how to live for Jesus, rejecting the worldliness of this life, living for others, never for themselves. They speak about it, only to do it all again next week, and the next…The buzz and enthusiasm engendered by such speakers in many churches is amazing. They say, "Come and bring your friends" and they do. They say, "Go out onto the streets" and they go. Alas, for some the commands become so briefly held. They grow little root in their hearts, and then are gone. The most precious gift which came at Christmas, the one to share with the world, stays hidden. We may have faith to move mountains, but without actions we are just bells clanging in the wind.

James asks very little of his reader: what is central in our lives and can we share it? For example, Monday morning arrives with the usual, "How's your weekend been?" Do we say, a) "Oh fine thanks," b) "Went to church," or c) "Had a really great time with my friends"? Why mention church first up? Jesus is a friend too. "We met and …" Unfortunately, many people run miles from saying the 'c' word (almost to Nineveh), sometimes finding it hard to share, a fact that James recognises.

James writes of what we're doing, using the word ἔργων. This is the Greek word for our 'works' or 'deeds'. As Christians our work is often what fills our minds and preoccupies our being. What are our thoughts immersed in? – In this Jesus, or, as James reminds us, in the worldliness around us? As we are us, it's likely to be a mixture of both, if we're honest. Being part of the body of Christ (the church), as James writes, is not being saved by what we do – it's being saved so that we can do things. To those around us with needs, we can show that we care just as Jesus showed care to the world he walked in.

James points out how we may do this (James 2:15-16): "Suppose a brother or sister is without clothes and daily food. If one of you says to him, 'Go, I wish you well; keep warm and well fed,' but does nothing about his physical needs, what good is it?" (Warmth, food, and clothing are basic needs, which our UK laws say we should not be deprived of). Yet non-Christians know how to give good things. "If you, then, though you are evil, know how to give good gifts to your children, how much more will your Father in heaven give good gifts to those who ask him!"

(Matthew 7:11). Jesus shows His Father wants to shower gifts on us His children, just like Christmas everyday! He cares so much for us, giving gifts to each according to their needs. Now, are we going to be selfish or are we going to share?

Giving gifts or care is a two way street. You give – I get. The idea is that I get what I need, not just what you can spare. Most people can spare a little of their change, which Jesus saw in action one day in Jerusalem: "He saw the rich putting their gifts into the temple treasury. He also saw a poor widow put in two very small copper coins. 'I tell you the truth' he said, 'this poor widow has put in more than all the others. All these people gave their gifts out of their wealth; but she out of her poverty put in all she had to live on'" (Luke 21:2-4).

Most people would never give away all they had, even if it does say in Acts that, "All the believers were together and had everything in common. Selling their possessions and goods, they gave to anyone as he had need" (Acts 2:44-45). Not everyone is called to give away all they have. Each of us however is called to perform different tasks or ministries, some as teachers, others as preachers, writers, givers, carers, - all sorts. But each and every one of us is called personally by Jesus. His call is one of caring for our world, just not all in the same way. As James reminds us, we are called to do something. To care like Jesus is like having Christmas everyday (because He shares).

<u>To you this Christmas blessing</u>

Cold hunger seeps through London's breath,
Hush stills, wants, passing phase,
Loosed o'er our earthen skies above,
Frosts winters eerie glaze.

In cardboard land they're hoping,
Whilst Park Lane crushes strife,
To herald our Christ's coming,
The harbinger of life.

A Christmas without presents,
No lights, no fairy tree,
Night watchers wait for endings,
Christ like it might well be.

To you this Christmas, blessing,
Smiles fortunes forgiving cares,
Spare thought for Christmas lonely,
The Christmas no one shares.

Everyone's called to do something. What might God be calling you to do?

Prayer

Father, there is so much poverty, debt, sadness, and loneliness around our world that I do not know where to start. Help me to see where there is something I can do. Send me as you sent James. Help me to make a difference where I live and work. Amen.

Memory verse

Romans 12:6a

We have different gifts, according to the grace given us.

Action

Is there someone you know, in or around your area, who might need either a little cheering up, or is in financial difficulties, or is out of sorts, and would like a Christmas present? I'm sure they wouldn't object if you couldn't find Christmas gift wrapping. Jesus came wrapped, but arrived as a helpless babe, as it's often more important what's on the inside.

Day 29

Doing the right thing today

Reading: Matthew 6:25-27

[25] "Therefore I tell you, do not worry about your life, what you will eat or drink; or about your body, what you will wear. Is not life more important than food, and the body more important than clothes? [26] Look at the birds of the air; they do not sow or reap or store away in barns, and yet your heavenly Father feeds them. Are you not much more valuable than they? [27] Who of you by worrying can add a single hour to his life?"

Meditation

Do we always 'do the right thing?' If we accidentally bump into a parked car, do we put a note under their wiper saying, "Sorry, call me?" When boarding a train, do we let the passengers off first or push on? If we know what we should be doing and don't, how does that leave us: forgetful, annoying, or anxious about getting on? Anxiety seeps into numerous areas of our lives, almost as background noise to our daily living. Always there, never quite forgotten, only missed when it stops.

We appear to spend so much time worrying about our lives. What to wear with those shoes. It's going to cost how much? You're planning on going where?!!! We miss the detail. It's not about what where we're going. It's about what we're doing right now, the here and now, not the there and then. 'Now' is the most important part of our lives. There may not be a tomorrow, so why worry? Do take precautions and prepare, but worrying just gives an excuse to live in tomorrow, ignoring today with its own special moments.

Matthew 6 has Jesus asking us a question. So tell me, what is tomorrow going to be like? It's like counting the raindrops in my hand. We don't actually know. We can speculate, dare I say 'like tomorrow', but we don't honestly know, not really, which is the point Jesus makes. How 'honest' are we being with ourselves? Occasionally perhaps deceiving ourselves of our abilities to know and control what's going to happen. By worrying about tomorrow we forget about today, or rather we ignore today and what's going on; we shun today's responsibilities, dismissing today's gifts from God.

I think the book of Proverbs (renowned for intrigue and curious quotes) has it when it comes to truthfulness: "An honest answer is like a kiss on the lips" (Proverbs 24:26). Which of us could refuse a kiss? But Jesus' question still stands: how honest are we about today's responsibilities? If honesty were measured by kisses, the lack of them might be a telling answer. We often live our lives in tomorrow, foregoing our chance to change today, even for a kiss.

Take hunger for example. Does it worry us that people around the world are hungry today and they're still going to be hungry tomorrow? What can we do today, if tomorrow they're hungry again? OK, perhaps world hunger's a bit big. What about locally where we are? If we walk around our streets, do we see hungry or needy people? I would dearly love to say no. Jesus walked the streets of Jerusalem finding multiple needs: spiritual, physical, and emotional, everywhere he trod. We see Him responding as they daily arose.

Spiritual needs
"I am the bread of life. Your forefathers ate the manna in the desert, yet they died. But here is the bread that comes down from heaven, which a man may eat and not die. I am the living bread that came down from heaven. If anyone eats of this bread, he will live forever. This bread is my flesh, which I will give for the life of the world" (John 6: 48-51). Jesus saw

inside the hearts of His listeners, seeing not just their hunger for physical food, sustaining for a few hours, but food to help them into His new kingdom. This same food is available to us. We don't have to queue up, just ask. Jesus provided more spiritual nourishment to this world in 30 or so years, than the world had seen since the beginning of its existence.

Physical needs

Jesus called his disciples to him and said, "I have compassion for these people; they have already been with me three days and have nothing to eat. I do not want to send them away hungry, or they may collapse on the way" (Matthew 15:32). Spirituality only takes us so far. If our bodies are pining for food, it gets in the way of everything else and needs satisfying. The crowd had been following him for three days. Now was the time for that miracle take-away. It's likely the crowd had food at home, but Jesus saw their presenting need where they were now, and fed them.

Emotional needs

Psalm 131:2 records, "I have calmed and quieted myself, I am like a weaned child with its mother; like a weaned child I am content." In the midst of a crisis, the Psalmist writes that he chose to compose himself, sensing how stressed he'd become. Jesus too knew anxiety: "After he had said this, Jesus was *troubled* in spirit and testified, 'Very truly I tell you, one of you is going to betray me'" (John 21:31). John uses the Greek word ἐταράχθη meaning to be anxious or concerned in our minds. Jesus shows His anxious mind again in the garden of Gethsemane. "He took Peter and the two sons of Zebedee along with him, and he began to be sorrowful and *troubled*. Then he said to them, 'My soul is overwhelmed with sorrow to the point of death. Stay here and keep watch with me'" (Matthew 26:37-38). Here the Greek word ἀδημονεῖν is used, meaning more anguish or depression. And in John 11:33: "When Jesus saw her weeping, and the Jews who had come along with her also weeping, he was *deeply moved in spirit* and troubled." John uses the Greek words, ἐνεβριμήσατο τῷ πνεύματι denoting that Jesus joins her in her sorrow and distress. He wants to be with her and part of her distress.

Jesus understands what stress is like and how it sometimes doesn't go. When He was anxious we see Him taking time out to pray, to still His mind, to pause in the day and see where He's at. It's perhaps this which is often missing from many lives, as people rush into tomorrow. It's about pausing in the day, stopping everything I'm doing and seeing what and who's around me, feeling where I am with what's going on.

Jesus' last recorded words on planet earth, according to John 19:30, were addressed to His Father. He said, "Τετέλεσται!" meaning to fulfil or complete. Jesus focuses on the day, because He sees today as important. What's going to happen tomorrow is tomorrow's, not today's. On one particular day, Jesus saved the world. On all the other days He fed the hungry, cured the lame, raised the dead, and did all sorts of other things. Each day has its place, one day at a time. Our task is to do the right thing at the right time, just as He asks us to do. We are to live one day at a time, as who knows what tomorrow might bring?

(OK, God knows all about tomorrow, but have we asked Him about it?)

Prayer

Father, in the rush of this world help me to still my racing mind and heart each day so that I may feel and sense your presence in my life. Show me how to live for the moment in the world you made for us. Help me not to ignore the needs of those around me. Show me where I can make a difference today. Amen

Memory verse

Proverbs 24:26

An honest answer is like a kiss on the lips.

Action

Find a time today to sit and listen. Be still, and hear the world rush around you. Then tell someone close to you what you've done, how you stopped rushing just for a moment and asked yourself: "Where am I at this precise moment? What's going on just this second around me? I'm me, and God created me for a special purpose today, the thing that He wants me to do today, which only I can do on this one day."

Day 30

The fruits of worry

Reading: Luke 12:22-26

[22] Then Jesus said to his disciples: "Therefore I tell you, do not worry about your life, what you will eat; or about your body, what you will wear. [23] Life is more than food, and the body more than clothes. [24] Consider the ravens: They do not sow or reap, they have no storeroom or barn; yet God feeds them. And how much more valuable you are than birds! [25] Who of you by worrying can add a single hour to his life? [26] Since you cannot do this very little thing, why do you worry about the rest?

Meditation

I'm told that 'deja vue' rarely occurs (except on TV and in the adverts). Today's passage is similar, almost, but not quite. This is tomorrow, which has now become today, hence we need to consider worry afresh. Today is full of yesterday's fruits. If we worried yesterday about today, this is what we've grown: worry fruits.

Fruit One: Independence
If we keep the worry to ourselves, it grows. If we do something about it, we may feel better. Do we share our burdens, ask for help, seek wiser minds than ours, speak to our minister or close friend? Not always. We're often solitary creatures. No sharing for us! We assert our independence, which is the first fruit of worry! I can do this myself, I'm in control. Unfortunately we cannot exist in isolation. We're created to be in community with other people: relatives, friends, work colleagues and

especially God. To deny our communities is to deny how God intended us to be, joined with others as God is united in the Trinity: Father, Son and Holy Spirit.

Fruit Two: Fear
Fear of what tomorrow may bring is the second fruit of worry. Horoscopes claim they show tomorrow. If you read them, what do you find? a) Something a little too vague; b) Contradictions; c) Similarities between different sign predictions; d) Double meanings; or e) Things we wish were true. Compare these with the Old Testament prophecies. God cared so much that He wanted to reassure us of what was coming, so all of these prophecies are spot on. By retaining our fear of tomorrow, we can end up deny God's promises for our lives. Fearing something says that it controls us, but recognising its influence helps us tackle it.

Fruit Three: Loneliness
Loneliness is the third worry fruit: the thought of no one intimately knowing me or me them. Returning home to a darkened empty house; sitting there as those around me continue to chat, excluding me; thinking who I can text that may text me back. For some, solitariness is strength, but others cry out inside: "Love me, care for me, even just see me sitting there and smile, please. Can I tell you how I feel, really feel? Can I say all the things I've never said, you've never heard or cared to hear, to someone who cares for me?" Once, Jesus was the loneliest man in the world, weeping the night before He died, as no one cared or listened to Him (Mark 14: 32-41).

Fruit Four: Indecision
The fourth fruit of worry is indecision. If you're a toddler, decisions can be a little limited, but if you're not, you need to decide. For example, Mat Man in Mark 2 had no qualms about what happened to him. Paralysed

and reliant on others, this was his lot, life on the mat. Only one day his friends decided to take him to Jesus, who characteristically said, "...get up, take your mat and go home." Life on the mat or freedom? Mmmmmm – tough choice. There's no half way ground with Jesus. Mat Man could have stayed on his mat, thinking to himself: "I'm not sure if I can make it in life off the mat, the mat's safer." Getting up, he walked away, or rather walked into his new life (with his mat). We can choose to remain on the mat, or to walk into our new lives. Alternatively, we could always ask for a fresh mat.

Fruit Five: Tiredness
Insomnia or tiredness is the fifth fruit of worry. Jesus was very good at sleeping. In Matthew 8:24, with waves about to sink the boat, what's Jesus doing? Sleeping! The disciples wake Him up saying (or more likely screaming), "Lord, save us! We're going to drown!" Jesus, roused from His slumber, rebukes the waves and probably (although the writer doesn't say) goes back to bed. The disciples were experienced sailors. If they were worried about sinking there was a problem. We may usually be quite good at sleeping, but it's that nagging thought that creates the storm in bed. Jesus shows us we need to deal with the problem. Otherwise it stays there and we sink. Get up and do something about it. Pray, write it down, talk to your partner, phone a helpline or an extremely good friend. Left alone we sink in our stormy lack of sleep.

Fruit Six: Stress
The sixth worry fruit is stress, coming from past or future worries: the 'why hasn't this worked out?' – our friends or partner's lack of care, God's lack of being there, or "I don't know, I'm just stressed." We may be finding it hard to comprehend why this is happening to us. Sometimes there is no answer, or no answer that we can accept – only misery. We find Jesus seeking help on numerous occasions from His Father, from

friends, from their friends, and from relatives. Jesus' ministry is full of asking for assistance: borrowing boats, places to meet, places to stay, food to share, donkeys, and coins to use. Asking for help can be the hardest thing to do. Sometimes there is no other way, as Jesus shows. We have to ask. Otherwise, we remain where we are – stressed.

Fruit Seven: Insecurity
Insecurity, the seventh worry fruit, is perhaps the most devastating, that sense of, "I can't do this, I can't cope, it's all too much." Our security should come from our trust in God, knowing we're loved and cared for by Him and by others. For some, security derives from what they own or have control of. Psalm 91 speaks about where our refuge is – our security. If it's not with God (who even may seem a bit absent in the stressful times) we may not be able to stand firm in the way that Peter admonishes us to: "Your enemy the devil prowls around like a roaring lion looking for someone to devour, resist him, standing firm in your faith" (1 Peter 5:8, 9). The devil still prowls around sowing seeds of insecurity, but flees with the prayer and support of God and our friends.

Worry Fruit Pruners
Worrying is not what God has in mind for us. He hopes for our lives to be filled with joy, peace, and love. His plans for us are occasionally thwarted by the worry fruits. We may worry when we feel our lives, relationships, jobs (or lack of them), or even ourselves, becoming too much. It's then we need a Pruner to snip away our worries. Pruners come in many kinds: partners, friends, relatives, person in the next pew, man on the bus home, secret pruners praying for us, and God the Master Pruner. God can turn us into Pruners too, using everything in our lives, even our own worries. He can make us Pruners, caring for those around us who are now growing worry fruits.

Are we ready to be a worry Pruner for someone we care for?

Prayer

Father, help me to hear your voice crying in my busy day. Direct my mind and thoughts as I decide my courses of action. Peel from me the worry and stress my world creates. Teach me to follow your ways. Show me how to rest in you, Lord Jesus, and in the love and care you freely give to me. Amen.

Memory verse

Proverbs 25: 27a

It is not good to eat too much honey.
- *We can have too much of a good thing, even honey!*

Action

We all worry and have concerns, though some don't like to admit it. Go and have a drink (and some cake) with your best friend, and ask them how they're feeling today. If necessary, read them some extracts from today's meditation, and see if they can relate to any of these.

Day 31

Waiting for the kettle to boil

Reading: Mark 8:35-36

[35] For whoever wants to save his life will lose it, but whoever loses his life for me and for the gospel will save it. [36] What good is it for a man to gain the whole world, yet forfeit his soul?

Meditation

For some, life ends in pain and suffering, whilst others slip silently away in their sleep. Different ends, yet all the same, our death. Our ways of life are equally divergent: joyful and fulfilled, hateful or troubled, a destructive terrorist, a contemplative monastic, a professional, a tradesman, the anonymous and quiet, the teacher, lawyer, or writer. Whatever we do, say, or become, at some point we end; recalled only by books, gravestones, or footnotes. Most are remembered fondly: good at cricket, not bad cook, OK for a drink. For others: "Not sure what they did. Worked in an office wasn't it – accounts? Anyway, what does the Will say?" With God there is never the anonymous, never the 'I'm not sure,' never the forgotten, but always the known and loved.

    The life most of us experience is one of relationships with others: partners, relatives, friends or lovers – the hermit life has lost its popularity. Those living with us tell us their life story, whilst influencing ours piece by piece as it unfolds before them. Watch it in their eyes as they discover where their life's going: the excitement of a university place or their first job. Watch the distress when they are sentenced for multiple armed robberies. Witness the happiness at the birth of their daughter, replacing the mourned loss of their son.

In our lives, whatever happens stays happened, no matter how awful. Even if we get our lives so messed up, God still has a plan for us, perhaps a different one from the one He originally wanted, but still a plan for everyone. Of course, we don't have to follow God or His plan. We can choose to walk away and live our own plan.

In God's plan, Jesus speaks about us losing our lives to gain them – what's all that about? He talks not of our physical death, but more a spiritual kind of death. Just like a physical death, it marks a finality – we are changed by it. If we lose our life or give our life to Jesus, we are changed by Him. We become dead to all the things we were, all that motivated us; instead we become born to how God would love for us to be. For some, this change comes in an instant. For others, it's a bit more gradual – they almost don't know they're changing until they have, changing minutely as God comes more into their lives – if they invite Him in.

There are points in our lives when we experience significant changes. God waits for these to happen, kind of like waiting for a kettle to boil. He sits waiting patiently till we're ready to change. God doesn't get annoyed waiting for us, as He loves us. We frequently get annoyed waiting for Him, demanding to know when it's going to happen.

"Where's the difficulty? I'm waiting, I'm ready now!"

We, like God, have to wait till we're ready for the change or task He wants us to do; to care, to say or to act at whatever at a point in time. God, and (I'm afraid) us, have to wait for the right moment, till the kettle's boiled. Have you ever tried to make tea with cold or lukewarm water? It's disgusting, all warm and wet. We have to wait till the water's boiled before we make the tea.

It's said everyone is called to something, but the 'calling' bit only takes you so far. Jesus called His disciples, but it took around three years before they had come to the boil, ready to serve God and care for His world. In calling we only begin to enter into a way of life. We don't become the 'whatever' till later. During our waiting, we're often bombarded by challenges as to where we're going, why we're doing it, and even doubts about ourselves and God's plan.

For some, the life they thought God called them to is not where He's now leading. This can be heartbreaking if we've set our minds on serving God in one way. Discovering He's other plans for us, the ones He had in the first place, which we've now come to recognise, because we've waited. Take for instance entering monastic life. It is one of those 'is this right for me' things. Throughout the journey to taking final orders (becoming a monk or nun) the person (novice) is asked the question: "Is this right for you?" Only for a few it is. For others, the 'rightness' of their journey lies elsewhere and they change direction. No one's rejected. It's just at that moment their life leads elsewhere. And this is what Jesus means about losing our lives to Him. We may have an idea about how we'd like to serve God, but He's got a better plan. We have to trust God wherever He leads us, which is incredibly hard. Often we have to wait till the kettle's boiled to see what we've turned out to be.

Discerning God's call may come to some as a bit of a shock. It did for Paul when he got blinded and for Samuel when he got woken all those times? Discerning God's call depends how good we're at listening. St Benedict, in his rule for life, begins the Prologue with the words listen, or harken. St Benedict wrote his Rules for a community of ordinary people, living and learning together, sharing the daily tasks of life for the benefit of all. To listen, as Benedict envisaged for his community, is to listen to God, His word, and those people who form our community. Without listening daily to these we cannot hope to find where God may be calling us to serve and care.

We may sit and wait for the kettle to boil, but once it has we need to know if we're making tea or coffee (instant or filtered). Our waiting is a time of discernment of God's plan, and preparation for our part in it; discerning where we're going by listening to God, His word, and our friends around us; asking them if it's tea or coffee, this job or that one, here or over there (not Nineveh please).

To lose our lives is to see ourselves transformed, to see what we've become when the kettle boils. Interestingly, water comes in three states: solid (when frozen), liquid, and as a gas (when boiled). It's still water, but can be used for different purposes, each separate and distinct from the other, but never together. Just as we are the same person, we can be used at different times for different things God has in mind for us. God has plans for us all, once the kettle boils.

Prayer

Lord, show me the life you would have me walk with you. Show me the path only I can tread, even the bits I would rather skip and ignore. Your path is one set for me. Help me Lord to bear the load you wish for me to carry, and help me to carry the load of others where they too need help. Amen.

Memory verse

Isaiah 41:10

So do not fear, for I am with you; do not be dismayed, for I am your God. I will strengthen you and help you; I will uphold you with my righteous right hand.

Action

Is there someone you know who would like a hand with something around the house, a chore or two they find it difficult or hard to do? Go and ask if you could lend a hand sometime, maybe today, or in the future.

Day 32

Being the bystander

Readings

John 5:2-13

Healing at the Pool

² Now there is in Jerusalem near the Sheep Gate a pool, which in Aramaic is called Bethesda and which is surrounded by five covered colonnades. ³ Here a great number of disabled people used to lie – the blind, the lame, the paralysed. ⁵ One who was there had been an invalid for thirty-eight years. ⁶ When Jesus saw him lying there and learned that he had been in this condition for a long time, he asked him, "Do you want to get well?" ⁷ "Sir," the invalid replied, "I have no one to help me into the pool when the water is stirred. While I am trying to get in, someone else goes down ahead of me." ⁸ Then Jesus said to him, "Get up! Pick up your mat and walk." ⁹ At once the man was cured; he picked up his mat and walked. The day on which this took place was a Sabbath, ¹⁰ and so the Jewish leaders said to the man who had been healed, "It is the Sabbath; the law forbids you to carry your mat." ¹¹ But he replied, "The man who made me well said to me, 'Pick up your mat and walk.'" ¹² So they asked him, "Who is this fellow who told you to pick it up and walk?" ¹³ The man who was healed had no idea who it was, for Jesus had slipped away into the crowd that was there.

Mark 2:1-12

Jesus Heals a Paralytic

[1] A few days later, when Jesus again entered Capernaum, the people heard that he had come home. [2] So many gathered that there was no room left, not even outside the door, and he preached the word to them. [3] Some men came, bringing to him a paralytic, carried by four of them. [4] Since they could not get him to Jesus because of the crowd, they made an opening in the roof above Jesus and, after digging through it, lowered the mat the paralysed man was lying on. [5] When Jesus saw their faith, he said to the paralytic, "Son, your sins are forgiven." [6] Now some teachers of the law were sitting there, thinking to themselves, [7] "Why does this fellow talk like that? He's blaspheming! Who can forgive sins but God alone?" [8] Immediately Jesus knew in his spirit that this was what they were thinking in their hearts, and he said to them, "Why are you thinking these things? [9] Which is easier: to say to the paralytic, 'Your sins are forgiven,' or to say, 'Get up, take your mat and walk'? [10] But that you may know that the Son of Man has authority on earth to forgive sins..." He said to the paralytic, [11] "I tell you, get up, take your mat and go home." [12] He got up, took his mat and walked out in full view of them all. This amazed everyone and they praised God, saying, "We have never seen anything like this!"

Meditation

If we've found something that's so fantastic and amazing, wouldn't we want to share what we've found? If that's Jesus, who can we bring to Him? Who do we care so much about that we want to share the greatest gift we've found? Who is it, and why have we not invited them before? Stopping the invite is occasionally the result of our own dithering, our failure to grab the moment, our procrastination. We've become bystanders to what we should be doing. Perhaps we are thinking what others will think about us or what we're doing, or we over consider the pros and cons, the 'consequences'. And then it's too late. Jesus and the moment have passed. (Well, almost, as Jesus keeps presenting us with more fresh moments, but then there's us dithering again). It's our human nature to dither. We ask questions, checking out what is best and questioning what is best and for whom.

If we're not careful (and thankfully most of us are), we could spend our days dithering about, thinking about ourselves, never quite making things happen. It's easy to spend our time thinking about how we can get through the next hour, what's for lunch, is it home time, is this sermon ever ending, or just watching TV. We're human, so we think about our needs first, the 'what will get us through the next half hour'. Dithering briefly for a moment is OK, but if we dither too much, we miss the Jesus moment. Jesus on the other hand is a doer, not a ditherer. When we read the Gospels we see Jesus separating the doers from the don'ters. He does take time out to relax with His friends, but He's there doing all the same, ever seeing the needs of others before His own.

Take a look at the numerous healings done by Jesus, accompanied by a slumber of bystanders. (I'm not sure of the collective noun for bystanders. You get mobs of kangaroos, a loveliness of ladybirds, and a slumber of sloths. Slumber seems to fit the bystanders). Not all, however, are 'standing by'. Some have brought friends for healing, or want healing themselves. Others are there to criticise, or to catch Jesus out with their 'clever questions'. They're just standing by waiting, certainly not doing.

In John 5 we find Jesus down by the Sheep Gate one Sabbath. Watching Him are the Jewish religious leaders, who criticise His healing and how He gets the man to carry his own mat! Why is it a crime for the man to carry his mat? Because carrying your mat on a Sabbath is work. Instead of criticising the bystanders for not helping the man into the pool for healing, Jesus gets moaned at for breaking religious 'mat carrying' legalisation. Interestingly, the Jewish leaders must have spent some time hanging out down by the Sheep Gate waiting for Jesus. What were they doing: dithering about, thinking of their own needs, certainly not helping the people by the pool in case of mat related code violations.

Take the friends of the man on the mat in Mark 2. They must have considered the lunacy of their actions: breaking through the roof of the house in broad daylight. "What will people think? What if he's not healed? What then? How do we get him out and what about repairing the roof?" And what about the unfortunate man on the mat? He must have agreed to this, but still may have questioned: "What if I'm not healed? What then? How do I get out of there? We're going be in so much trouble if this doesn't work."

Mark doesn't provide the pre-house breaking discourse, the arguments beforehand. Jesus is here, now is the time, so let's do it before He moves on. There's one chance. Mark does record the strange incident: Jesus is teaching, there are a few questions from the audience, then there's this most awful noise from the roof with bits of it beginning to fall in. There's now light coming through and faces looking down, and here's a man on his mat. What on earth is going on? Jesus knows and steps forward. It's extreme, yet it works because this is the only way to share Jesus with the man on the mat.

Certain TV shows advise viewers not to try at home what they see on the screen, and in this case they're right, but only so far as the roof breaking bit. Jesus teaches that nothing should stop us getting our friends to Him, certainly no dithering around, not even a roof should stop us. If taking the roof off is the only way for someone to find Jesus, then that's the way. Who said preaching and sharing the gospel was dull when you get to take a roof off once in a while?

Each part of Jesus day was seeing then doing, not dithering. It was not a matter of what they could do for Him, but how He could care for them, and how He could make their lives brighter as He passed through. Who cares what others think? This man can now walk. Which is better: his walking, or my social standing?

Consider Jairus' daughter from Luke 8:51. The place was packed out with people wailing and crying. What does Jesus do? He shoos them out and calls the girl back from death. What about the man born blind in John 9:1? Here we have the man's neighbours and friends watching, with the Pharisees standing by to criticise, but Jesus is doing the healing and caring.

Jesus challenges us over how we think and live for Him. He looks at what we're doing with the time we have. Are we 'standing by' as bystanders, or doing the doing? We all may sometimes say, "It's too big, it would never work, there's too many obstacles". It's easier to cross the road and pretend they don't exist, avoid eye contact, and pretend the problem isn't there. It may be easier, and in many instances it's what may happen, but the problem's still there. There's still the man by the pool needing help, lying paralysed on his mat.

Sometimes we can only stand and watch as there is nothing we can do. We will be bystanders. At other times, Jesus is standing there asking us whether we are bystanders or by-doers.

Prayer

Lord, show me where I can serve, where I can be the catalyst making a difference. Help me to be your light in the darkness. Show me where there is a need I can change. Thank you Lord for all of my life, especially where I'm not too good at things. Help me to use all my experiences to change the world around me. Amen.

Memory verse

Matthew 11: 28

"Come to me, all you who are weary and burdened, and I will give you rest."

Action

Do you know someone who's unwell, in hospital, or in need of a chat or text? Why not contact them to see how they're doing and whether you could pop in to see them.

Day 33

Is God real or was I mistaken?

Reading: Psalm 22:1-2

¹ My God, my God, why have you forsaken me? Why are you so far from saving me, so far from the words of my groaning? O my God, I cry out by day, but you do not answer, by night, and am not silent.

Meditation

How do we feel when God seems so far away?

Perhaps it always was just me, God the illusion, me the reality. When feeling alone, we may believe that there is just me, abandoned, in a state of mind unshared. The question is, who's moved from who – us or God?

In being alone there exist two opposites: solitude and isolation. One is a gift from God, the other a curse not shared, no matter how the pain sears.

Our beloved moves away, they turn and look, and we sense their words, not their love: goodbye, no more, we've broken up. There is no longer 'us'. What did I do? How could I have loved you more? My heart and love once yours, lie pierced and broken on the floor. We are no longer one, we've become forsaken, isolated – something which Jesus too experienced, as did King David, God's favoured one, who cried out in Psalm 22: "Where are you, what have I done, I'm sorry already. Forgive me." God seems absent, or perhaps there is no God in the first place, just me.

Sometimes we almost sense words of doom before they come, sitting there as the conversation leads to a truth moment. The words are said, they're real: "You did this, on this, with…, did you not?" Then it's passed and there is no more we can say. It's done, the end, what now? Fear grips us. We are alone. There is no God, just me, and my guilty shame.

As Jesus dies, He turns to the guilty and, taking their shame upon Him, says, "I tell you the truth, today you will be with me in paradise." No one is forgotten or forsaken in isolation. It is never too late to say we're sorry. Even if our wrongs bring us to execution, Jesus is there waiting for us, taking our guilty shame.

Each of us is known, each is loved, just as each is tempted into wrongs. We sin and make mistakes, yet we remain loved by Jesus, because we're intimately known by Him. David in another anxious Psalm moment writes: "Search me, O God, and know my heart; test me and know my anxious thoughts" (Psalm 139:23). When dying, Jesus turns to the guilty man, and it's as though He says, "Come be with me, I love you as no other can."

And yet God seems far away from us.

Isolation first sprouted in a garden between two lovers and God. "Where can we hide from God?" said one to the other. They'd tried, but God kept asking where they were. They hid, and still He asked, "Where are you?" Realising their guilt, they appear before Him: God has searched and found them naked in their shame and guilt, and yet He loves them. In another garden, Jesus, God's Son, beckons to us saying, "I still love you. Come back to me. I will take your guilty shame."

God knows we hide from Him – we've done it before. Sometimes we don't even realise we're doing it, perhaps wishing to be alone, or feeling a need for solitude. Other times our lives become too much and we run from our fears, hoping to hide from suffering. We're ashamed of what we said, our actions and thoughts locked in battle, hate flooding our minds. And still God searches for us.

We may too hide from God the pretence our lives feign to be, hiding to protect ourselves, too scared to discover who we've become. We hide, and still God comes searching: "Where are you?"

> Then the man and his wife heard the sound of the LORD God as he was walking in the garden in the cool of the day, and they hid from the LORD God among the trees of the garden. But the LORD God called to the man, "Where are you?" (Genesis 3:8,9).

Adam and Eve hid from God, as they feared what they had become – shameful in God's eyes.

> If I go up to the heavens, you are there; if I make my bed in the depths, you are there. If I rise on the wings of the dawn, if I settle on the far side of the sea, even there your hand will guide me, your right hand will hold me fast. If I say, "Surely the darkness will hide me and the light become night around me," even the darkness will not be dark to you; the night will shine like the day, for darkness is as light to you (Psalm 138:8-12).

God is everywhere. His presence permeates our whole planet. There is nowhere to hide where God is not. Still the isolation continues. Who's moved – us or God? If God no longer cared, He would not search or seek us out. We would be abandoned, declaring, "There is no God. I was mistaken. There is no Jesus nailed to a cross turning to a convict saying, 'To day you will be with me in paradise, come I forgive you. Return to me for I love you.' There is no God searching and rejoicing when He finds us. God no longer cares. There is only us – just us. I was mistaken."

The fool says in his heart, "There is no God." They are corrupt, their deeds are vile; there is no one who does good. The LORD looks down from heaven on all mankind to see if there are any who understand, any who seek God (Psalm 14:1-2).

And yet God still loves and cares for us.

It does not matter if we believe or not God is caring. That's our choice. Around our world, good is happening, people do care, love is shared, misery broken. Even amongst the isolation.

Consider this: If there was no God to care, we would not find anyone else caring either. To care or love someone, we need a model to copy, an example. Some things we could never dream up ourselves, no matter how many evolutionary jumps we make. Survival of the fittest is not about how I can help you. Our moral code derives not from a Godless society, but from one where God is present. A truly godly culture shows us what is good and evil, unlike the evolutionary or natural selection theories which cannot 'select' or develop a moral code of good and evil.

Is God real, was I mistaken? Real enough to come back to, or real enough to know Him in the first place? God cares enough to search me out, to take my guilty shame. How can I show this same care to my neighbours?

Prayer

Father, forgive me where I do not see you in the world around me. Forgive me when I forget to include you in my plans for the day. Forgive me when I do not ask you what is best for me. Forgive me when I ignore you and forget to pray. Instil yourself in my heart Lord, and how you would have me be for you and for the world around me. Amen.

Memory verse

Mark 12:27

"He is not the God of the dead, but of the living. You are badly mistaken!"

Action

Is there someone you know who does not believe in God, but has been asking you questions about Him? Go and have a chat with them about their views, and see where it takes you.

Day 34

Being obedience

Reading: 2 John 1:1-6

¹The elder, to the chosen lady and her children, whom I love in the truth – and not I only, but also all who know the truth – ² because of the truth, which lives in us and will be with us forever: ³ Grace, mercy and peace from God the Father and from Jesus Christ, the Father's Son, will be with us in truth and love. ⁴ It has given me great joy to find some of your children walking in the truth, just as the Father commanded us. ⁵ And now, dear lady, I am not writing you a new command but one we have had from the beginning. I ask that we love one another. ⁶ And this is love: that we walk in obedience to his commands. As you have heard from the beginning, his command is that you walk in love.

Meditation

Every day the same: up, work, home, eat, TV, bed, start again. Dullness personified? See outside this into life's routines: we are creatures goaded by routine, positives and negatives. If it works, we're more likely to do it again, irrespective of circumstances. Routines are frequently challenged, stemming our creativity, personal advancement, and social interaction. We do the same as we did yesterday – nothing changes. Correct, but who are we doing it for?

As Jesus walks beside a lake, he sees two fishermen, brothers in fact (Simon and Andrew). He says to them, "Come, follow me, and I will make you fishers of men" (Matthew 4:19). The work routine has not changed. Instead of catching fish, they're now catching people (kind of the same) for God's Kingdom. The skills were already in place. It just needed Jesus to channel them to new and exciting heights. So it is with us. The necessary caring skills are already imbedded. We do care deeply or otherwise for the needs around us. We just need, as Homer Simpson says, "A little help please" to see them blossom. But I have Jesus in my life already. He's my help.

Having Jesus in our lives and obeying Him are distinctly different things. Caring should be an obedience to Jesus' way of caring; not the version that our culture poses as obedience. With Jesus' obedience comes the discipleship cost, which the original disciples discovered all too painfully. To follow Jesus is to give your life away, literally. Making these disciples, as Jesus found out, is not an easy thing (as it's us).

Jesus knew His disciples well: squabbling, forgetful, sleeping everywhere, the worries and denials, the love for Him, occasionally wavering or totally denying him. These were the twelve He chose to change the world, no back-up plan, this will work! We too, as His disciples frequently fall short of His expectations, which is part of discipleship, as we keep trying to get it right. It's called routine.

Jesus knew the value of routine, teaching His disciples as they travelled with Him to live as He did. Pray like this: "...go into your room, close the door, and pray to your Father who is unseen" (Matthew 6:6); Work like this: "As you go, preach this message: 'The kingdom of heaven is near.' Heal the sick, raise the dead, cleanse those who have leprosy, drive out demons" (Matthew 10:7-8). Live like this: "Nobody should seek his own good, but the good of others" (1 Corinthians 10:24). Routines provide frames for us to survive and grow in. Where a life lacks routine, it lacks direction, and the owner drifts.

Our choices give direction, and like the choice of Simon and Andrew open possibilities: "At once they left their nets and followed him" (Matthew 4:20). This was not their first encounter with Jesus. He was there the day before and they'd got to know him. (John 1:35 records,

"Jesus was there again the following day"). Today, now, was decision time. Do we follow Jesus or stay where we are? If you asked them, I'm sure they'd have no regrets.

They brought with them their routines, an ordinariness of life, which is the same for us. Jesus calls us, with our ordinary ways, our routines. Why me? I'm far too dull, too ordinary. It is in the ordinariness of life that Jesus cares. Jesus calls the ordinary, to become extraordinary for Him. Look at how Simon (later Peter) fared when Jesus entered his life. The loud boldness of Peter is channelled into being a fierce advocate for Jesus. He's still the same Peter, this time obeying Jesus, not his own whims (well most of the time). He's doing what he always did, standing up and saying (usually shouting and arguing), "Let me tell you about Jesus." His missionary work is recorded in Acts 8 to 10: travelling from Jerusalem to Samaria, Nazareth, and Antioch, then into Caesarea, preaching and teaching.

Jesus saw the potential in Peter. Peter could have said no. He could have stayed with his boat, watching Andrew walk away with Jesus. Peter's choice, just like Jesus' call to care, is a free choice. We can stay, watching Jesus walk away without us. We can stay in our life's safe routines, Jesus-less, but that's our choice.

What does Jesus offer? He offers an ordinariness we already have, but this time with potential to rock the world, or at least our own neighbourhood. Peter realised the importance routines offer as he accompanied Jesus. With Jesus constantly showing him and the other disciples how to live their lives through prayer, meditation, discussion, love, and care. If Jesus can change Peter, a somewhat loud boisterous individual, prone to rushing into things, often without considering what he wants to do next, He can change each one of us, through practice, through our routines, into carers for Him.

Just why is obedience so hard for us today? Obedience is not a natural human state, just as service grates against our free will. "If I do that, they'll take advantage of me." If I'm obedient I lose control, if I'm in charge it's my decision. Obedience is hard because we lack the patience to practice. Jesus encourages us to practice obedience, doing as He does. Even His disciples managed it (with a little help from God's Holy Spirit). We too should, pondering Jesus' life, letting it seep into our own, becoming part of our routine.

Jesus said, "It's just like this, ... who comes to me and hears my words and puts them into practice. He is like a man building a house, who dug down deep and laid the foundation on rock. When a flood came, the torrent struck that house but could not shake it, because it was well built. But the one who hears my words and does not put them into practice is like a man who built a house on the ground without a foundation. The moment the torrent struck that house, it collapsed and its destruction was complete" (Luke 6:47-49).

Our lives in Jesus are founded on practising what builds us up, the ordinary routines that make us into the caring people Jesus wants us to be.

How much is caring part of our routine? It was central to Jesus' routine and that of His disciples, with "a little help."

Prayer

Father, help me to hear Your call in my life. Still my heart so that I can hear You speaking to me and guiding me. Show me the path You have set for me, and help me to walk it as Your obedient servant. Where there are challenges which seem too great, comfort me, so that I in my turn may comfort others with the same love that I receive from You. Amen.

Memory verse

Isaiah 1:19

If you are willing and obedient, you will eat the best from the land.

Action

Who lives next door to you? Who do you see regularly when you're out shopping? Could they do with an evening doing something different with you and some of your friends?

Day 35

The onward Christian struggle

Reading: 1 Corinthians 1:26-31

[26] Brothers, think of what you were when you were called. Not many of you were wise by human standards; not many were influential; not many were of noble birth. [27] But God chose the foolish things of the world to shame the wise; God chose the weak things of the world to shame the strong. [28] He chose the lowly things of this world and the despised things – and the things that are not – to nullify the things that are, [29] so that no one may boast before him. [30] It is because of him that you are in Christ Jesus, who has become for us wisdom from God – that is, our righteousness, holiness and redemption. [31] Therefore, as it is written: "Let him who boasts boast in the Lord."

Meditation

Jesus sat looking at His sleeping disciples, wondering about them making a difference. He was thinking, "It's going to be hard being a Christian in 20 years time. In 2000 years it's going to be even worse. Their friends will think they're weird and there's all that post modern spiritual stuff to deal with. They'll certainly think I'm too old, and as to what's happening now – all the things this lot are going to write about. The sceptics will laugh their heads off when they read it, but I can't wait to see their faces when they find it's all true." Smiling he whispered "Go Christians Go." "Ooops! They don't get that phrase for another 2010 years, but they'll love it." Note to self: Get alarm clock for sleeping disciples.

For many of us, our Christian lives today are an effort. Our beliefs are challenged, questioned or belittled. Jesus is right, living as Christians today can be hard, even in a western society. We may wrestle with our beliefs when relatives say we should give up this Christian nonsense. Or perhaps we're shunned, made fun of at work or school, because we stand up for Christian values. Others just struggle in following their Christian beliefs, with doubts they made the right choice to follow Jesus in the first place. Our struggles comprise three parts: what's happening, our feelings, and how they affect us.

Struggle Audit

What's happening: obstacles in our way, disrupting our lives and preventing us from doing things, creating doubts.

Our feelings: upset, inadequate, sad, in pain, frustrated, motivated, determined?

How they affect us: challenge us, help us think through an issue, show us what we can achieve, help us discover more about Jesus

Struggles are with us till the day we die. It's part of our humanity; we question things. For some the exertion seems quite overwhelming, others grow within their struggles. Still others flounder, reaching a point of despair crying out for help. In all our personal struggles and the struggles of those we love, there is a nagging doubt of God's remoteness. No one is without that, 'I'm not sure' moment.

Jesus looked at Peter, so peacefully asleep, no doubt thinking of the struggles he would have when he denied Him three times. Peter will be inconsolable.

God chooses us for His tasks (doubts and all), just as He chose Peter. He chooses us not because we're necessarily good at something. It's just that we're the right person. "Why me?" we ask as we tussle with our lives. It's because of our struggles and the way we manage them. God asks us to do something. That's why God chose us. We may believe we'll never be good enough, except with God the possibilities simply explode. God chose the foolish things of the world to shame the wise; God chose the weak things of the world to shame the strong (1 Corinthians 1:27). We're here because God knows what we can do. He's placed us here just for the job, because he knows we can do it, just us, only us.

Our responses too can be a bit of a battle: "Should I? I'm not sure I'm up to it. What if it goes wrong?" We already are responding. God uses what we may count as insignificant, to bring care and relief, dispelling suffering through our endeavours with life. Few of us are without Christian scuffles. They're either part of us or we see them around us.

It takes three to struggle: the struggler (the person having the awful time), the strugglee (the person trying to help), and the strugglist (the person who helps the strugglee). We are not alone in our grapples, as Peter and the other disciples discovered. They and we are found by Jesus, no matter where we got to. Jesus, when He finds us, performs a struggle audit (see above).

We may not like our own personal conflicts, but God uses each one to show care for His world. In struggling we see how we can care for others who, like us, are in the midst of their own battles. Everyone strives. Few may openly admit just how much they do. Others show it on their faces or in their behaviour. It is in our wrestling that we come face to face with Jesus and His own struggles.

We know suffering is with us, and we know that God does not always intervene as we would like (another frustration for us to cope with). Suffering remains, no matter how much we pray and strive to care. There are times when nothing seems to be happening and we don't know the answer. Is our world itself too corrupt? Are we seeking healing where there is none, looking always for the positive side of God and maybe not His suffering side? We look, and sometimes we do not see how we can make a difference. Sometimes we create suffering through our reluctance or inability to intervene. In the midst of the struggle, the pain and the hurt, there is Jesus, and we ask the question, "Why does God not intervene?" Sometimes we do not know.

To those of us who do intervene, no matter how small our contribution, the difference is profound. Lives are changed, suffering is stemmed, pain averted and care shared.

Prompted by God we can change the world, through our everyday actions of caring, our tiny little interventions. These can rock the world. It's sad to say that our world does not always see it, and there too is suffering. To say that God does nothing in allowing the suffering, is to remain outside of what God can do in touching ours lives so that we too can touch others with the love and care we receive.

Jesus took another look at the sleeping disciples. "The world better watch out," He thought, "This lot, and all the ones to come, are going to rock the planet." Feeling satisfied, he too fell asleep.

Prayer

Father, thank you for your understanding and love in my life; thank you that you care for me and are concerned about what I'm doing. Teach me how to see the good in those around me and the potential inside them. Help me to encourage them as they grow and develop. Help me to share with them what I have found in you. Amen.

Memory verse

Psalm 23:4

Even though I walk through the valley of the shadow of death, I will fear no evil, for you are with me; your rod and your staff, they comfort me.

Action

Do you know a Christian who is struggling or going through a rough patch? Ask them round for an evening meal, to pray and chat about what's going on in their own walk with God.

Day 36

Being busy to care today

Reading: Mark 12:28-34

The Greatest Commandment

[28] One of the teachers of the law came and heard them debating. Noticing that Jesus had given them a good answer, he asked him, "Of all the commandments, which is the most important?" [29] "The most important one," answered Jesus, "is this: 'Hear, O Israel, the Lord our God, the Lord is one. [30] Love the Lord your God with all your heart and with all your soul and with all your mind and with all your strength.' [31] The second is this: 'Love your neighbour as yourself.' There is no commandment greater than these." [32] "Well said, teacher," the man replied. "You are right in saying that God is one and there is no other but him. [33] To love him with all your heart, with all your understanding and with all your strength, and to love your neighbour as yourself is more important than all burnt offerings and sacrifices." [34] When Jesus saw that he had answered wisely, he said to him, "You are not far from the kingdom of God." And from then on no one dared ask him any more questions.

Meditation

Phone Rings. Hello? ………………….. (Not again, why me, isn't there anyone else who could help them?) Yes I'd love to. When? …………….. Oh sorry, I'm busy then ………………….. Of course, maybe later, if no one else ………………….. Bye.

It's not that we make excuses. Sometimes we are too busy helping somewhere else. We fill our lives, or perhaps we allow our lives to become filled. We choose to shift the importance ratings to fit how we spend our time.

Jesus had this question of importance posed to him by a religious legal teacher. Note the difference in his attitude: he saw Jesus had already given the other questioners 'good answers'. So his question was not a hostile one, but one of genuine concern: How do we see the needs around us?

The law teacher's reply shows he ranked his loving responsibilities: God first, then care for His people. Jesus acknowledged his insight. Seeing the man had answered wisely, He said, "You are not far from the kingdom of God." To pricritise our time is perhaps the hardest task we manage, as life crowds in with its constant changing demands. Jesus' recognition of time management speaks volumes to us today, asking – how well do we manage our time for God? If we love God and our neighbour, we are not far from the Kingdom. One small step is needed. How do we see that needy neighbour amidst our busyness? Perhaps by making sure we've not become over busy to care?

If I fill my days with God's work, surely that's me keeping His commands. Yes? Well it is a 'Yes', but it's a 'No' too. It's not that I'm doing the wrong thing, but am I doing what God wants me to be doing, right now? Have I checked, just to make sure? In our busyness we need to pause, confirming this is how God wishes us to spend our time just now. Usually it's the "Yes, go for it!" but the pause to pray allows God to nudge us, perhaps tightening the focus on what we're doing, just a little.

How do I tell? Is there some kind of criteria for choosing? Strangely, Jesus says there is. Who do you love the most: you, your neighbour or God? Just as you love yourself (and we all do), love God, then love your neighbour as yourself – our 'loving criteria'. Jesus shows this in practice as He cares for and heals His own neighbours: "Jesus went throughout

Galilee, teaching in their synagogues, preaching the good news of the kingdom, and healing every disease and sickness among the people" (Matthew 4 23), all interspaced with prayer. We need to ask, "Am I on the right track? Does this need a little re-focusing?"

What helps stop the busyness?
Our own busy days like those of Jesus are filled with all kinds of chores. These need doing, as Jesus the carpenter knew all too well. You cannot run a carpentry shop without having to clean it, make repairs, check your stock, do the paper work, and chuck the rubbish out. It's the timing of when we do these that Jesus asks us to consider – He certainly had to. It's not that I don't have time, but when will I do what needs doing, and is now the right time to do it?

Best equipped to care
For Jesus, time is important, as too is having the right tools for the job. It's no use trying to cut a tree down with a teaspoon. We need to be equipped for the job; here with caring tools. Listening, encouraging, seeking, being there, noticing, challenging, loving, admonishing, washing, making, asking, giving, telling.

Being equipped to carry out something involves actually being on the receiving end too, as Jesus found out. Jesus the carer had needs. When He's being crucified, His followers are standing there waiting to care for Him in death: Mary Magdalene, Mary the mother of James and Joses, and the mother of Zebedee's sons (Matthew 27:56). In Galilee these women had followed Him and cared for His earthly needs (Mark 15:41), later covering His dead body with spices ready for burial. Throughout his life Jesus had known care, from His Mother as a young child, to the hospitality shown to Him as He travelled. Caring for others is just one half of the caring equation. The other is allowing care to be shown to us. Peter too found this out, late one Passover night (John 13:6-9).

Like all skills, caring skills need to be practiced and sharpened for readiness. But what if my care is rejected? Most of us take rejection personally, it's our humanity. Rejection amounts to three stages. First, it's me being offended – my care is not wanted. Then there's the person I'm caring for saying, "That's not really what I had in mind, more this." Lastly, instead of seeing the care we're offering as being rejected, we feel personally rejected (even if only for a tiny moment).

Does Jesus care about rejection? Mmmmmm ... He's been there too many times. "The stone the builders rejected has become the capstone" (Mark 12:10). "He who listens to you listens to me; he who rejects you rejects me; but he who rejects me rejects him who sent me" (Luke 10:16). As Jesus hung dying on His cross He called out with a loud voice, "My God, My God why have you forsaken me?" Rejection can be personal, as Jesus knows. If we're rejected, might we not need some care? "Do not let your hearts be troubled. Trust in God" (John 14:1). Our Father, who sees our inner selves, knows how we hurt when we care for His world. He knows what we do to make a difference. We can trust God to keep us free to care, in the way He wants us to care, amidst our busyness.

Prayer

Lord, show me where I've become too busy. Forgive me when I've said no once too often. Help me to see where I can make a difference, even just a small one. Thank you Lord for the opportunities you give me in my life, to share your love with those around me. Help me Lord to be your hands and feet where I am. Amen.

Memory verse

2 Chronicles 15: 7

"But as for you, be strong and do not give up, for your work will be rewarded."

Action

When was the last time you took some time off from work or from being concerned about other peoples' issues or problems? Today, go and find a friend and have a chat to them about how you feel about working or caring. See what reaction you get from them. Would they like to help you (with the caring) or at least pray for you and some of the things you're doing?

Day 37

Fearing the unexplainable: the consequences of caring

Reading: Mark 5:11-20

¹¹ A large herd of pigs was feeding on the nearby hillside. ¹² The demons begged Jesus, "Send us among the pigs; allow us to go into them." ¹³ He gave them permission, and the evil spirits came out and went into the pigs. The herd, about two thousand in number, rushed down the steep bank into the lake and were drowned. ¹⁴ Those tending the pigs ran off and reported this in the town and countryside, and the people went out to see what had happened. ¹⁵ When they came to Jesus, they saw the man who had been possessed by the legion of demons, sitting there, dressed and in his right mind; and they were afraid. ¹⁶ Those who had seen it told the people what had happened to the demon-possessed man – and told about the pigs as well. ¹⁷ Then the people began to plead with Jesus to leave their region. ¹⁸ As Jesus was getting into the boat, the man who had been demon-possessed begged to go with him. ¹⁹ Jesus did not let him, but said, "Go home to your own people and tell them how much the Lord has done for you, and how he has had mercy on you." ²⁰ So the man went away and began to tell in the Decapolis how much Jesus had done for him. And all the people were amazed.

Meditation

The problem with buying a new car (besides choosing the colour) is if something goes wrong, unlike our old one, we often don't know how to fix it. Today it's all onboard computers and dual this and that. It's outside our experience (or at least mine). Second hand ones come with a history of niggling, yet understandable, issues. Even if we can't fix it ourselves, at least we can understand the problem. We like to know what we're getting into, the possible outcomes and the consequences, but with caring we don't always know what these may be.

One of Jesus' gifts to us is sorting out our needs. His care is freely given, in the hope that we'll share what we've received. When it stops with us, remaining as an unopened Christmas present, forgotten, unshared, the gift is lost to the world. All that's left is a gift of sadness; a sadness in Jesus' eyes we've not shared His present to us, His Father's love. To those of us on the receiving end of care, what can we do? Share what's been shared with us, as Jesus commands (Mark 5:19). Sometimes it's not that easy – I'm physically or mentally unable; other times there are consequences.

Jesus knew all about having His care rejected, a kind of love in adversity. "Then the people began to plead with Jesus to leave their region" (Mark 5:17). It's as though they're saying to Him, "Thank you for not continuing to care, please leave." Jesus faced perhaps one of His greatest tests here when they said, "Go away." He arrives, with disciples in tow, at a predominately Gentile area, having just quietened the stormy journey across lake Galilee. As they land they're approached by a man possessed. The man, knowing his need and seeing the cure (Jesus), asks for and receives healing. The response from the rest of the town is, "Go away, you're not welcome." Getting back into the boat, Jesus and the disciples do, leaving behind the cured man.

The town didn't like it: "A healing here? Whatever could happen next!?" Perhaps the villagers felt they'd done all they could for the man – they were caring for him already. Jesus' healing was too strange for them. It was outside things they could, or more likely the things they didn't want to, engage with. They were frightened of the power Jesus represented, and what He might do next. For some of us, the experience of healing may be something quite strange. People aren't healed today – we're far too modern.

The consequences of something new, the inexplicable, may be outside our experience. And here we have choices: accept them for what they are, reject them as outside our comprehension, or deny they ever happened. Please choose ☺

Just like buying a new car, if something goes wrong we can either reject the problem (as we don't understand it), deny there is a problem and try to carry on using it, or take it to a mechanic who sorts out it out, telling us what's wrong so we learn about our new car. We're no longer frightened of getting it fixed, because we understand a little more about it. Just as with healing, some people are sceptical of healings happening today, or frightened, as they do not understand where they come from. They tell us (and Jesus) to go away, as they fear the consequences of someone being healed. They fear the power behind healing, because they do not understand, or perhaps don't want to understand: "Whatever could happen next?"

Jesus is only carrying out what His Father showed Him to do. "As the Father has loved me, so have I loved you" (John 15:9). Jesus asks us to do what He's been shown by His Father. Jesus' earthly father loved him and taught him a trade. Jewish boys were taught a trade irrespective of who they were. Paul, the writer, knew how to make tents! Likewise Jesus' Heavenly Father showed him His love and what He had to do with it. In Jesus' own words: "I have made you [God] known to them, and will continue to make you known in order that the love you have for me may be in them and that I myself may be in them" (John 17:26).

Perhaps we're a bit afraid to care, to step into the unknown. Imagine a world without care. We'd have the "Who cares – not me!" principle. Not an opposite of caring – more an absence of caring – one that promotes selfishness. It would be all about me, and certainly not you. "I don't care about you. Go away!" As Jesus walked around Palestine, He frequently encountered this attitude. "I don't care. Go away. Leave us alone." He was shunned by those He came to serve, sometimes even before he got there: "[He] sent messengers on ahead, to a Samaritan village to get things ready for him; but the people there did not welcome him" (Luke 9:52-53). Knowing He would be rejected didn't stop Jesus caring, in fact it made him more earnest to show His love and care to them: "But I tell you who hear me: Love your enemies, do good to those who hate you" (Luke 6:27).

Jesus' caring is one of acceptance of the person and their needs. He wants to assist them, but He is not saying that you have to have what's offered. It's your choice. "If you choose not to accept, I still love you, but I will move on." We may meet people who we'd love to help, but they're not ready yet, or others who do not want what Jesus is offering. When Jesus returned to Heaven, there came the gift of the Holy Spirit to us, bringing discernment of how and when to care.

Caring, as Jesus found out, often means rejection. Pray for them and move on. We too, who are called to show Jesus' love, will meet rejection. Pray for them and move on, not forgetting to shake the dust off your feet as you leave (Mark 6:11).

Prayer

Lord, teach me how to be more tolerant to the people I meet and work with. Help me to see their good side, even in the midst of frustrations or arguments. Show me how You are using each of them in building up Your Kingdom. Lord, help me to be accepting of help, not shunning assistance when I do not look for it, but welcoming help and the person helping me. Amen.

Memory verse

Proverbs 19:20

Listen to advice and accept instruction, and in the end you will be wise.

Action

Go and ask for some help from someone whom you would not usually seek help from. Tell them what's on your mind and ask them if they could help you solve this, or at least some part of it. Sit and chat about this over tea or coffee, asking them how they're getting on in their walk with God.

Day 38

We too can walk on water

Reading: Matthew 14:29-31

[29] "Come," he said. Then Peter got down out of the boat, walked on the water and came toward Jesus. [30] But when he saw the wind, he was afraid and, beginning to sink, cried out, "Lord, save me!" [31] Immediately Jesus reached out his hand and caught him. "You of little faith," he said, "why did you doubt?"

Meditation

Most of us walk on water every day, quite innocently, by the faith we have in Jesus Christ – a faith providing for our needs and building us up into who God would have us be. When life goes wrong (or seems a bit much), the water suddenly appears deeper than we thought, and our insecurity cries out: "Save me Lord, save me!" We've stepped outside our securities, and realise as Peter does that we too are sinking.

We also sink because we're trapped in our comfy zone, our routines have taken over, or our boat's over full of fish (we're doing too much). "They caught such a large number of fish that their nets began to break ... and filled both boats so full that they began to sink" (Luke 5:6-7). Comfort zones, however, do need stretching from time to time. If not, they become our prisons. It's only comfortable as long as we know we can leave, if we wish, by getting out of the boat. We may get wet, but we can jump back in. Just like a baby kangaroo (Joey) leaping in and out of their mum's pouch. If we never jump out, the pouch remains our prison.

And like most prisons or pouches, it may need challenging, just in case we've got stuck inside.

We also need to check every so often that we're not hiding inside our comfort zone. For instance, when was the last time we thought about visiting someone we didn't know, or getting involved in a visiting scheme to a prison, a care home, or a local psychiatric unit? "I was hungry and you gave me nothing to eat, I was thirsty and you gave me nothing to drink, I was a stranger and you did not invite me in, I needed clothes and you did not clothe me, I was sick and in prison and you did not look after me" (Matthew 25:42-43). Would we visit them and clothe them? Would we … really?

Would we be too afraid to go, afraid of stepping outside our comfortable caring zone, afraid of caring where we've not cared before, afraid of trying something new in the caring line? Would we get out of our comfortable boat, to see what the water's like in the lake of unknown caring? Often it's a bit cold at first, but then it warms up and feels OK as we swim around. Once we've tried something new and we find it's OK, it feels right doing it. "Then the righteous will answer him, 'Lord, when did we see you hungry and feed you, or thirsty and give you something to drink? When did we see you a stranger and invite you in, or needing clothes and clothe you? When did we see you sick or in prison and go to visit you? And the King will reply, 'Truly I tell you, whatever did for one of the least of these brothers and sisters of mine, you did for me'" Matthew 25:37-40).

What if we do leave our comfy zones? Isn't there a risk of drowning, or at least getting wet? "Immediately Jesus reached out his hand and caught him" (Matthew 14:31). Jesus is there waiting to catch Peter, and us too. Just before this, Peter the fisherman (who should've known better) has jumped out of his boat and he's in the middle of a lake. What's he doing, getting out of a moving boat? This is madness. The cost for him was his faith in Jesus. Would he float, or would he sink?

Not until Peter takes his eyes off Jesus and becomes afraid does he sink – because that's what happens if you get out of a boat in the middle of a lake and take your eyes off Jesus. Jesus reminds us of the necessity to keep ourselves close and focused on Him – otherwise we sink. The fear of, 'I can't do this' often prevents us stretching ourselves in God's work and doing something new. It can prevent us from caring, wherever and to whoever that may be (even in the middle of a lake). Staying in the boat (the safe boat), we don't get wet. Getting out and risking ourselves we may get wet, but never drown. Jesus promises to save us, even in the middle of a lake – there's already a precedent.

These sinking feelings may come when we're not sure what we should be doing, or how we should be caring. What if, in all our efforts to care, we get it wrong, we mess up? Reassuringly, Jesus doesn't rebuke. Instead He asks a question about our lives, "How salty are you?" "You are the salt of the earth. But if the salt loses its saltiness, how can it be made salty again? It is no longer good for anything, except to be thrown out and trampled by men" (Matthew 5:13). It's about whether we are making a difference. Has what we've done changed another's life for the good? Are we still willing to change the world by our actions? Are we still salty? Jesus knows we get it wrong all too frequently. This is why He is waiting there, ready to save us when we're out of our boat, afraid and drowning.

What of the care we give without even realising we're doing it – perhaps a smile, a handshake, a hug, a tactful word, or just our presence? We don't dive in – we sit and listen, we pray, we hold their hand, we cry with them, we listen with them to the silence around us. We care as the situation dictates, because that's what is needed. "There is a time to listen, a time to die, a time to mourn and a time to heal" (Ecclesiastes 3).

Having jumped out of our boat, what of us as carers and how the caring affects us? We do get worn out, tired, irritable about caring (and the person we are caring for). We get frustrated that the care we offer is not accepted, or seems not to be the care they even want, such as when they've shouted that they hate us (again) and it's the dementia talking – not them anymore! "I'm caring here," we scream, "what more do you want of me?" John 13:6 and 7 holds an answer. He [Jesus] came to Simon Peter, who said to him, "Lord, are you going to wash my feet?" Jesus replied, "You do not realise now what I am doing, but later you will understand." The care we offer is sometimes misunderstood or unaccepted. We can only do what we think is right, what we believe to be in the person's best interests. Jesus speaks to Peter, He sees beyond the foot washing, right into Peter's life.

For some, caring is giving irrespective of how others treat us. Sometimes they may be unable to understand what's needed. They may have lost their mental ability to know what's best for them, or perhaps have a condition preventing them saying what they'd like. Here we should care about what is best for them, guided by how we feel Jesus would have cared.

If we are to be water walkers, we need to see how far we can walk from the boat. We should get out and test the water. Even if we then decide to get back into the boat, at least we've had a try. We may get horribly wet as we walk the water, but Jesus never promised us an easy journey, or a dry one.

Prayer

Lord, help me get out of my boat and walk the water with You. Show me where I can test out new areas of what I can do with my life, even if only stepping out of my comfort zone briefly. Show me where Lord. Thank you for the opportunities you have given me to walk the water Lord, and forgive me where I've huddled in my boat. Open my eyes to see others who are water walkers, and help me follow their example. Amen.

Memory verse

Matthew 14:31

Immediately Jesus reached out his hand and caught him. "You of little faith," he said, "why did you doubt?"

Action

Is there someone in your church, club, work place, school, or wherever you find yourself, who you've never spoken to before? They may be new, not really your type, outside your usually friendship group. Go and say hello and have a chat about how their day (and yours) is going.

Day 39

Receiving love and care from others

Reading: Luke 17:11-16

Ten Healed of Leprosy

[11] Now on his way to Jerusalem, Jesus travelled along the border between Samaria and Galilee. [12] As he was going into a village, ten men who had leprosy met him. They stood at a distance [13] and called out in a loud voice, "Jesus, Master, have pity on us!" [14] When he saw them, he said, "Go, show yourselves to the priests." And as they went, they were cleansed. [15] One of them, when he saw he was healed, came back, praising God in a loud voice. [16] He threw himself at Jesus' feet and thanked him – and he was a Samaritan.

Meditation

I love you for what you did for me, thank you. ☺ xxx

We don't always express our love for someone when they help and care for us. This may be caused by embarrassment, fear of rejection, ignorance, or we just forget. We may wish to express our love, but can't find the words to say we love them. We don't know how they'll react, or even if we should express our love to them at all.

Only one leper comes back to Jesus to say thank you. What of the other nine lepers? ('Leper' here denotes a medical condition feared by the ancient world, resulting in all who developed it being cast out from their communities). Did they not love the person who healed them of this awful condition? They can now rejoin society, be accepted, and have friends again in their community. What lives did they go on to lead? Where did they end up? What were they like? Unfortunately, Luke only records that they were healed and walked away.

Loving others (because they cared enough to love us first), is littered with reasons why we sometimes don't thank them for caring for us.

Leper 9: The shyness of love
If I hide my feelings about how I was cared for, who benefits? – No one. "Nothing in all creation is hidden from God's sight" (Hebrews 4:13). Knowing that everything I do is in God's sight and subject to His control, allows me to show the hidden love that I feel for someone who cares for me. Even if I try to hide my love, it comes out eventually. "There is nothing concealed that will not be disclosed, or hidden that will not be made known" (Luke 12:2).

Leper 8: The fear of rejection in love
Saying to someone who cares for me, "I love you and want the very best for you," for some opens possible rejection. We've said it before and had it thrust back at us. God never rejects what we do in His name, because He loves us. "Praise be to God, who has not rejected my prayer or withheld his love from me!" (Psalm 66:20). In Him there is no fear. I can feel secure in what I do, if done in His name and with His purpose in mind. "There is no fear in love. But perfect love drives out fear, because fear has to do with punishment. The one who fears is not made perfect in love" (1 John 4:18).

Leper 7: Defending love
Having once been cared for by someone, only to then lose them, is too painful. Do I want to tread that path again? They cared so deeply for me,

we trusted each other. We loved and cared for each other. But then I lost them, they died. I'm alone, defenceless, marred. "Because he loves me," says the LORD, "I will rescue him; I will protect him, for he acknowledges my name (Psalm 91:14). I do not love you, I cannot love you, but I will care for you; please accept what I can offer, for this is all I can give. Asking for honesty brings healing in both directions. "Better is open rebuke than hidden love" (Proverbs 27:5).

Leper 6: Intellectualising love
Can love be academic, an intellectual exercise unadorned with passion? I want your care, not your beliefs. Caring sometimes demands that we are like Jesus, caring in a world that rejects the very nature of Jesus and His love.

Leper 5: Time for love, unselfish love
A time for wisdom, a time for love, a time for denying one's self, a time to say goodbye to self. Sometimes caring seeks inside us a space to hide reality away. For some, caring brings them too close to how one day they too may be. "Let love and faithfulness never leave you; bind them around your neck, write them on the tablet of your heart" (Proverbs 3:3).

Love and selfishness can join forces for the benefit of the carer and those they serve in love. "Rather he must be hospitable, one who loves what is good, who is self-controlled, upright, holy and disciplined" (Titus 1:8).

Leper 4: Deceptive love
I know that person – they cared so much for me. I never knew that side of them, what their past held secret. Let God forgive them as I do. "When Judas, who had betrayed Him, saw that Jesus was condemned, he was seized with remorse and returned the thirty silver coins to the chief priests and the elders. 'I have sinned,' he said, 'for I have betrayed

innocent blood.' 'What is that to us?' they replied. 'That's your responsibility.' So Judas threw the money into the temple and left. Then he went away and hanged himself." (Matthew 27:3-5)

Leper 3: Missed opportunities of love

I had such a short time to live. The hospice cared. Thank you. My family, I'm sure they came, surly to visit me. They must have, definitely, yes. "Therefore, as we have opportunity, let us do good to all people" (Galatians 6:10). We have but a short time, time to do both good and evil. We can please ourselves and no one really cares. "At one time we too were foolish, disobedient, deceived and enslaved by all kinds of passions and pleasures. We lived in malice and envy, being hated and hating one another" (Titus 3: 3). Or we can please other people with care. One day we will consider our life's events, our big adventure – those disappointing regrets, the missed smiles, and moments and silences never filled.

Leper 2: Love in an empty world

The world hates me, but you it loves. There is no reason for its choice. You cared – I hated you. You succeeded and I failed so many times. I loved, and lost my love in anguished pain. It is a godless world; no prisoners taken. There is no relief. I want to stop, please, but then you've won. To this comes Jesus with one message: come have my love and hope. Strive to share my love and hope with a lost and forgotten world. The world may not see, but it feels your love and care. The difference is us. "In the same way, good deeds are obvious, and even those that are not cannot be hidden" (1 Timothy 5:25).

Leper 1: Not interested in love

Phone rings ... "Hello, I'm fine thank you, no I don't want any, good bye." "I have no one else like him, who will show genuine concern for your welfare. For everyone looks out for their own interests, not those of

Jesus Christ." (Phillipians 2:21-22). Even if I give my time, my energy away for free, it is still not accepted by some. What more can I do to help them? It's free, what else can I do? "If the world hates you, keep in mind that it hated me first" (John 15:18) – *Jesus Christ Son of God, 1st Century, Palestine.*

"I love you." "Do you?" "Let me show you."
"Love is patient, love is kind. It does not envy, it does not boast, it is not proud. It is not rude, it is not self-seeking, it is not easily angered, it keeps no record of wrongs. Love does not delight in evil but rejoices with the truth. It always protects, always trusts, always hopes, always perseveres" (1 Corinthians 13:4-7).

"Do you really love me that much?" "Yes, I love you that much." "What – really love me?" "Yes, I love you." "Love me that much?" "Yes, that much; thank you, love you." ☺ xxx

Prayer

Thank you Lord that there are people who care for me. Thank you that they show this care to me even if I don't feel or know about it. Thank you Lord that there is someone praying for me in the world right now. They may not know my name or anything about me, yet still they pray for me. Thank you Lord for my education, my home, and my possessions; thank you Father that you love me. Amen.

Memory verse

Jesus raises Lazarus from the dead

John 11:41

So they took away the stone. Then Jesus looked up and said, "Father, I thank you that you have heard me"

Action

We all do it. We forget to say thank you or to show appreciation for what someone's done for us. Is there someone you would like to thank for something in your life? Text them, email them, write them a short thank you note or card, phone them and say thank you.

Day 40

Jesus the deliberate king

Reading: Matthew 21:1-11

The Triumphal Entry

¹As they approached Jerusalem and came to Bethphage on the Mount of Olives, Jesus sent two disciples, ² saying to them, "Go to the village ahead of you, and at once you will find a donkey tied there, with her colt by her. Untie them and bring them to me. ³ If anyone says anything to you, tell him that the Lord needs them, and he will send them right away." ⁴ This took place to fulfil what was spoken through the prophet: ⁵ "Say to the Daughter of Zion, 'See, your king comes to you, gentle and riding on a donkey, on a colt, the foal of a donkey.'" ⁶ The disciples went and did as Jesus had instructed them. ⁷ They brought the donkey and the colt, placed their cloaks on them, and Jesus sat on them. ⁸ A very large crowd spread their cloaks on the road, while others cut branches from the trees and spread them on the road. ⁹ The crowds that went ahead of him and those that followed shouted, "Hosanna to the Son of David!" "Blessed is he who comes in the name of the Lord!" "Hosanna in the highest!" ¹⁰ When Jesus entered Jerusalem, the whole city was stirred and asked, "Who is this?" ¹¹ The crowds answered, "This is Jesus, the prophet from Nazareth in Galilee."

Meditation

What happened the last time you met a King? – A lot of bowing and less chatting? For the rest of us who've never meet one it's a worriment in waiting. What do you say to a King or a Queen? "Hi, how're the servants getting on?"

At Passover, Jerusalem seems to be gathered to meet lots of kings, or at least people who thought they were kings. It is unlikely the occupying Romans would've have tolerated a parade openly acknowledging a king's arrival in Jerusalem. So what do we see here? Another person royally greeted by the crowds, or someone deliberately entering with His disciples and subtly fulfilling the messianic predictions about Him for those who can read the signs?

Jesus' entry into Jerusalem riding on a colt was deliberately planned, a bit of prophecy fulfilling. "Rejoice greatly, O Daughter of Zion! Shout, Daughter of Jerusalem! See, your king comes to you, righteous and having salvation, gentle and riding on a donkey, on a colt, the foal of a donkey" (Zechariah 9:9).

Matthew 21:7 records, καὶ ἐπέθηκαν ἐπ' αὐτῶν τὰ ἱμάτια: and they put upon them (the colt) the (their) garments. Other people, ἔστρωσαν ἑαυτῶν τὰ ἱμάτια ἐν τῇ ὁδῷ: spread their garments in the road (Matthew 21:8). The rest of the crowd is cutting leafy branches from the nearby fields and spreading these on the road. Considering the value of the garments they're using, this is an amazing royal welcome.

However, it's not what Jerusalem wanted. They sought a king, a military fighter to banish the Roman threat. What they got was a servant showing care to the world, riding in on a colt covered in other people's coats. Coats seem nothing special until you examine the fashion conscious disciple.

The wardrobes of AD 33 were singularly unlike those of today. Today many of us have drawers dedicated to t-shirts, others for tops, cupboards for dresses and skirts, many over stuffed with the latest fashions and accessories. And usually several coats, matching our favourite outfits. In AD 33 you had one coat. If you lost it, or gave it away, you got cold (OK very cold). Unless you applied Exodus 22: 26 and 27, you stayed cold. "If you take your neighbour's cloak as a pledge, return it to him by sunset, because his cloak is the only covering he has for his body. What else will he sleep in?" If you're dead or about to die you had no further need for clothing. Clothes were so valued that even the soldiers cast lots for Jesus' garments. The care shown to Jesus when He entered Jerusalem is stripped away as He dies.

The crowds came seeking a king, but they got a Saviour, a Saviour deliberately showing Himself to Jerusalem (if you knew what to look for). Like the crowds, there are times when, although we look, we fail to see the obvious. They stand there unadorned; this is my need, will you not help me? It's not what I'd like – it's what I need to survive. Our own prejudices and wants perhaps prevent us seeing the reality standing before us.

Jesus arrives advertising who He is. Here is the Messiah – take it or leave it. The Jerusalem entry is proclaimed, yet all but a few miss it. It's likely the Pharisees (the Jewish leaders) didn't miss who'd just arrived. They knew the prophecies too. Sometimes we do miss who's right in front of us. The woman selling magazines we don't really want, the man playing so badly he needs lesson's, or the poster with the baby smiling (we hope they're smiling, not grimacing from starvation). And we're walking on by – we didn't notice (or noticed and needed to walk a bit faster).

What did the crowd see as the Saviour of the world entered Jerusalem? Did they see a man on a donkey, another crucifixion victim, or something in it for them? It's likely the latter. Joining in with the disciples the crowd shouted "Hosannah! Hosannah!" thinking how Jesus would change Jerusalem for them. They too perhaps didn't see the Saviour of the world arrive.

Jesus' arrival stirred up the Pharisees. "Some of the Pharisees in the crowd said to Jesus, 'Teacher, rebuke your disciples!', 'I tell you,' he replied, 'if they keep quiet, the stones will cry out'" (Luke 19:39-40). Jesus offers the Pharisees another chance to accept who He is. Don't they see the signs? Don't they see who's before them? Quite obviously not; they too don't see, and walk on by, criticising Jesus and His disciples, later plotting His death, hoping to end this little uprising. Once He's dead that'll be the end of Him and them! (Mmmmmm ... said how many years ago?)

And what of us standing in the Jerusalem crowd waving our palm branches? Or standing today in church with our neatly folded 21st century versions? How are we responding to Jesus riding into Jerusalem?

There is one last part of Jesus' entry that's occasionally forgotten: Jesus the Commander. "Jesus entered Jerusalem and went to the temple. He looked around at everything, but since it was already late, he went out to Bethany with the Twelve" (Mark 11:11). Why enter Jerusalem so late in the day, have a quick look around and go? It makes no sense. Particularly as He's back in the morning throwing the temple furniture around; why not do it now, as we're here, save some time, give us a free day tomorrow, a bit of sight-seeing?

Here we see Jesus with His twelve disciples still in tow. He's not lost anyone; equally, they have not deserted Him. They are still loyal to Jesus. They arrive in Jerusalem proclaiming to those who see, this is the promised Messiah. Were the disciples beginning to see what might happen, how events were likely to unfold. Possibly they did and yet here they are entering Jerusalem beside Jesus, thinking "Is He going to His death?" They may desert Him later, but for now they're with Him and encouraging others. Like all Commanders Jesus knew that His men (and Himself) needed rest. He looks around, and then retires to Bethany for some peace before mounting His campaign in Jerusalem. Jesus is in command of what's happening. These were not random events. Each was planned and prepared with exact precision.

We see Jesus in control; He leads His disciples as he leads us, with this same skilled precision. To care, to love, to touch, to give – Jesus the

King is in control, no matter what may happen. What happens is our choice, but what orders might Jesus the Commander give us today?

Prayer

Father, open my eyes to what's happening around me, the things I would so dearly like to ignore. Help me in my misunderstandings and where I do not see that I could make a difference. Show me what I can do, even small changes that help another's life to be just a little better. Lord, if you want to send me, use me or my possessions, show me what You have in mind for my life. Amen.

Memory verse

Psalm 118:22

The stone the builders rejected has become the capstone.

Action

Is there one item of nice clothing that you do not need, something sitting at the back of the cupboard? It's been there for a little while and is just there, no longer worn by you. Go and find a charity shop you can give it to.

Day 41

Furniture hurling

Reading: Mark 11:15-19

Jesus Clears the Temple

¹⁵ On reaching Jerusalem, Jesus entered the temple area and began driving out those who were buying and selling there. He overturned the tables of the money changers and the benches of those selling doves, ¹⁶ and would not allow anyone to carry merchandise through the temple courts. ¹⁷ And as he taught them, he said, "Is it not written: 'My house will be called a house of prayer for all nations'? But you have made it 'a den of robbers.'" ¹⁸ The chief priests and the teachers of the law heard this and began looking for a way to kill him, for they feared him, because the whole crowd was amazed at his teaching. ¹⁹ When evening came, they went out of the city.

Meditation

Have you ever wanted to get that annoyed in church, perhaps during a PCC or other committee meeting (some can be quite frustrating), or found yourself thinking, "Why can't we just do it? What more is there to discuss?"

That day in Jerusalem Jesus was not in the throes of uncontrolled anger, only showing how much he cared for worship in the temple. He detested the blindness of the religious leaders to temple practices, and was forcibly reminding them it was still a place of worship. It's as though He's saying, "What are you doing treating it like a shopping precinct!?"

Some may be hesitant to challenge, but not Jesus. He's confronting and quoting in His usual style, two diverse sets of Hebrew scripture. Interestingly, one is aimed at Gentiles, the other at the Jews. Mark only records Jesus saying (as He breaks up the early morning shops), "My house will be called a house of prayer for all nations" (Isaiah 56:7).

The full context of this verse is Isaiah 56:6 and 7: "And foreigners who bind themselves to the Lord to serve him, to love the name of the Lord, and to worship him, all who keep the Sabbath without desecrating it and who hold fast to my covenant, these I will bring to my holy mountain and give them joy in my house of prayer. Their burnt offerings and sacrifices will be accepted on my altar; for my house will be called a house of prayer for all nations." Is Jesus looking into the future, seeing not only Jews coming to know him as the Messiah, but Gentiles too? Jesus shows that His love and care extend to all nations so everyone may know Him, not just the Israelites.

Jesus' remaining criticism comes from Jeremiah the prophet: "'Has this house, which bears my Name, become a den of robbers to you? But I have been watching!' declares the Lord" (Jeremiah 7:11).

Jeremiah 7 start with a discourse about Israel: "Hear the word of the Lord, all you people of Judah who come through these gates to worship the Lord ... Reform your ways and your actions, and I will let you live in this place" (Jeremiah 7:2,3). And verses 9 and 10: "Will you steal and murder, commit adultery and perjury, burn incense to Baal and follow other gods you have not known, and then come and stand before me in this house, which bears my Name, and say, 'We are safe, safe to do all these detestable things?'"

This is where the furniture throwing comes from. Jesus shows it's not just this Israelite generation who are forsaking God's commands – it goes way, way back. God's loving care knows no bounds. As He is eternal, His love and care for us exist both backwards and forwards in time, correcting and nurturing throughout the centuries. He is the ultimate 'Lord of Time'.

So – back to furniture hurling. Imagine we threw church tables around. What sort of reaction would we get? Most churches would be screaming "Stop!" Others might deeply question our sanity. All would look and wonder why we're doing it, exactly as they did with Jesus. Except with Jesus there's this acceptance of what He's doing. There are no guards arresting him; no calls for restraining orders or ASBOs. OK, the temple's a bit of a mess, but He's back the following day questioning the chief priests and teachers again. What did they think about this when plotting and scheming His demise? "They began looking for a way to kill Him, for they feared Him" (Mark 11:18). It's that sudden realisation moment: "Oh *&*!!$@?!!! – we've been found out!"

This is not the only lesson going on that day. We find the furniture hurling sandwiched between fig tree cursing (Mark 11:12-14, 20-21).

On first reading this incident, it doesn't seem to fit with Jesus' personality at all. Why curse a fig tree – is there something we've missed about them? But if we take this as a parable, albeit enacted, it makes perfect sense. Jesus approaches the fig tree, which is full of leaves, expecting some fruit. Having searched amongst its leaves, He finds there's nothing at all, not a fig to be had. Here is the heart of this parable: it's about expectation, in this instance from God. It's about what He's expecting from us.

Our ministries usually involve us in doing something: giving time, giving money, caring, shopping (for others), fixing things, giving car lifts, or sharing our stuff (maybe too a little furniture hurling). If the ministry we've been given is fruitless, God will want to know the reason why; as the cursed fig tree demonstrates. What use is a fig tree full of leaves and no figs? It might as well be cursed to the ground, for all the good it's doing – likewise the person who's been given a task or ministry. If they're full of talk and no actions, what use are they? They might as well be cursed to the ground!!! (...well, not actually cursed, as Jesus loves us too much), but you see the point.

God gave Jesus a task to perform that day: furniture hurling, and we see Him very much in action. God gives each of us a task, sometimes equally exciting as furniture hurling. Often it's more ordinary, but equally vital in a 'hurling' kind of way. God sees the whole jigsaw picture, but we only see the tiny bit which is our task, the one He asks us to do. The jigsaw still comes together, even if we don't do our bit. It will just look a little different when finished.

Jesus said, "I am the vine; you are the branches. If a man remains in me and I in him, he will bear much fruit; apart from me you can do nothing" (John 15:5). We are known by our fruits, being recognised by what we do. "By their fruit you will recognise them" (Matthew 7:16). If we're not following what God asks from us, have we become a fig tree, all leaves and no fruit? Casual observers may think we look OK, until Jesus comes along and points out what we're doing – growing leaves not fruit.

How fruity have we been today?

Prayer

Father, show me where I can be your furniture hurler, where I can stand up and say, "This far and no more!" Place me into situations where my words and actions can be used for Your work. Help me to be confrontational where I need to be, yet loving and gentle in everything I do. Amen.

Memory verse

John 15:5

"I am the vine; you are the branches. If a man remains in me and I in him, he will bear much fruit; apart from me you can do nothing."

Action

(I would dearly love to say, "Go and hurl some furniture," except perhaps I mustn't.) Today, instead of hurling some furniture, are there disputes where you are, or things that no one talks about? Are there people who do not get on with each other – family, friends, loved ones? Read them a little bit of today's meditation and see what they think about Jesus getting annoyed and His furniture hurling.

Day 42

Frustration and love

Reading: Matthew 21:28-31

The Parable of the Two Sons

[28] "What do you think? There was a man who had two sons. He went to the first and said, 'Son, go and work today in the vineyard.' [29] 'I will not,' he answered, but later he changed his mind and went. [30] Then the father went to the other son and said the same thing. He answered, 'I will, sir,' but he did not go. [31] Which of the two did what his father wanted?" "The first," they answered.

Meditation

> ***Scene One – Heaven (Discussion)***
>
> "What you up to today"
> "I'm busy!"
> "What you doing?"
> "Busy alright!!!"
> "Busy doing what?"
> "Stuff!"
> "What stuff?"
> "You know, saving the world stuff!"
> "Oh that stuff, why didn't you say?"
> "I'm busy, doing the stuff!"

Not an everyday heavenly conversation, but who knows? If we're prompted by Jesus, our lives contain a busyness for Him. We're all busy, seeking the way directed by God for our lives. We're praying to know where the next turn will take us. We're busy, "Doing stuff!"

As our days fill up with tasks, we need to ask whether we are filling them, or God is filling them. It's easy to be busy doing all kinds of stuff, letting things occupy our time. The question is: have we rushed into 'doing' things, leaving out the 'searching and checking this is God's will' bit. Do we rush into the first (or second) thing which pops into our minds, saying that this must be God's work, and then we're off doing it?

In the reading we see two dilemmas, one for each son. One refuses (we'll call him 'the Refuser'), then goes and helps. The other promises, (we'll call him 'the Promiser'), then stays put. Which of these two is more worthy of his father's praise? The answer naturally is the first, but why?

The Refuser (first son) says, "I'm too busy to go, I've got more important things to do than go to your smelly vineyard." Here is his dilemma: "I'm too busy." Other things crowd his life preventing him doing what is best for him. He may not appreciate it, but his father does. God does not ask us to do things just for the sake of it. There's a purpose, a reason why He asks. He asks it only of us, because we're right for the job. No other can do it. It's a privilege to be asked.

And then the Refuser changes his mind, "Perhaps I will go, it's not that bad a job." We've all done this. We've all changed our minds, perhaps not over jobs – seeing someone, making purchases, doing homework, or even choosing vocations. A change occurs in our thinking. How come we change? For that we have to look at the other son, the Promiser.

The other Sons dilemma (the Promiser) is that it's so easy to say yes, even when it's something you don't particularly want to do. Saying yes is almost programmed into young children. "Go and get Mummy's handbag. Can you find Daddy's torch for him?" Nothing wrong there, but eventually comes the "NO!" day, usually very loudly so the neighbours will hear. We say "NO!" as our freedom of choice arrives. We realise we don't have to if we don't want to, so we don't. Why should we? "I'm busy doing stuff!"

Promisers are busy too, often serving in communities or doing all kinds of work for God. However there's a 'but' (perhaps not a nice one). They may work for God, but how much of what they're doing is their choice, and how much are they doing because they feel they have to (and they'd feel guilty if they didn't do it)? God gives us freedom of choice. We don't have to do what He says, it's our choice. This freedom of choice is developed through understanding ourselves and our own self perspective.

Self perspective is how we see ourselves in relation to others. It matures through evaluating ourselves and what we're doing. As this grows we may shift the focus of our lives ever so slightly. God may move out of the spotlight and we ourselves begin to creep into the limelight as we slowly come to depend more on ourselves than on Him. We reach a point where we say "'I' can do this! Wow, look at me, I'm good at this – where can 'I' do some more?" 'I' may become our focus, our proud self becoming the centre of our life. God still gets to play a part in our life, perhaps second string, or the very least first reserve.

Now imagine a third son, 'the Doer'. Doers get things done, yes? They often know what they're good at, so they do that, usually very well indeed. It is a gift from God, doing what we're good at. We may be very good at organising, doing the admin, helping people, sorting out or moving the projects on – we're busy doing what we're good at. Now here's a question for Doers: how sensitive are you to those around you? Our own proficiency occasionally leaves others wondering, "Why can't we do that too?" In all our own doing, there's someone struggling to keep up with our wonderful examples. God loves our work because He gave it to us, but with this comes a responsibility to encourage those around us to strive to be the best they can. Not our best, but their best.

So we have our two sons, with an adopted third one: the Refuser, the Promiser, and the Doer. And which are we? Most of us maybe are all of them, but not all at the same time – often moving between them ever so subtly. There are, however, some who seem to be in one mode all the time: refusing, promising or doing. But that's how God made us and what makes up our communities. We are a body, full of different sorts of people with different parts, but equally loved and valued, as 1 Corinthians 12:14-20 records:

> Now the body is not made up of one part but of many. If the foot should say, "Because I am not a hand, I do not belong to the body," it would not for that reason cease to be part of the body. And if the ear should say, "Because I am not an eye, I do not belong to the body," it would not for that reason cease to be part of the body. If the whole body were an eye, where would the sense of hearing be? If the whole body were an ear, where would the sense of smell be? But in fact God has arranged the parts in the body, every one of them, just as he wanted them to be. If they were all one part, where would the body be? As it is, there are many parts, but one body.

It's not recorded if the father in the passage subsequently disliked either of his sons for their reactions or behaviour. Most parents would say that's what you get with children: frustration half the time and love the other half. What's strange, or perhaps not, is that's how God often sees us. He still loves and cares for us no matter how we work. But is this how we treat other people? Are we loving and caring towards the people we're working with?

Prayer

Father, are there parts of my life which need more of Your presence or Your power in them to change me? Open my eyes to what's going on in my life, things I'm pretending didn't happen, or areas which I need to revisit and consider afresh with You. Help me to understand what needs to be changed in my life to bring me closer to You Lord. Amen.

Memory verse

Matthew 18: 3

"I tell you the truth, unless you change and become like little children, you will never enter the kingdom of heaven."

Action

Make a list of all the things you are doing for others, and ask yourself these slightly hard questions. Why you are doing these things? Is what you're doing helping them? How could you improve what you're doing? Is the person you're helping growing in faith and independence, or have they become over reliant on you?

Day 43

Worthy to care - a life for Jesus

Reading: Philippians 1:27-30

[27] Whatever happens, conduct yourselves in a manner worthy of the gospel of Christ. Then, whether I come and see you or only hear about you in my absence, I will know that you stand firm in one spirit, contending as one man for the faith of the gospel [28] without being frightened in any way by those who oppose you. This is a sign to them that they will be destroyed, but that you will be saved – and that by God. [29] For it has been granted to you on behalf of Christ not only to believe on him, but also to suffer for him, [30] since you are going through the same struggle you saw I had, and now hear that I still have.

Meditation

'Wish you were here' is perhaps the epitaph of most holidays, even the wet ones. We write to our recipients out of duty and love, "Having a wonderful time, wish you were here, lots of love ..." No we didn't, it was awful. They weren't here with us, we missed them, and that's why we write it. Paul too is thinking of those he misses as he lies captive in Rome. "Tell me, tell me everything, so I too may share in your struggle." Writing to both thank and encourage the Philippian church, he reminds them of his commitment to their welfare and care. "Write and tell me how it goes, listen carefully to what I say".

Paul is the ever vitalising encourager, owing to his own 180 degree life experience. Have you ever asked for directions and been told, "It's that way, where you've just come from"? And with that sunk feeling, we walk back through everything we'd so triumphantly marched past. Saul (later Paul) was in this position when he realised he'd walked the wrong direction in life: "Saul was still breathing out murderous threats against the Lord's disciples" (Acts 9:1). Paul says of himself, "For you have heard of my previous way of life in Judaism, how intensely I persecuted the church of God and tried to destroy it" (Galatians 1:13). Paul met Jesus and continued meeting him. In our own lives, turning aside from our previous ways and walking in the other direction can only be done with Jesus, 'a daily Jesus', as Paul discovered.

It should be a daily walk with Jesus. It's no good topping up at the beginning of the week. It must be daily walk, just like watering my plants, one step at a time. We choose which way we step, backwards or forwards. It's a daily walk which Paul knows all about as he writes with enthused encouragement to everyone he's met. He writes, seeking more than a postcard back: "Tell me, tell me everything, so I too may share your struggles. I care, outside what is happening to me. Share yourselves with me, so I too may encourage you, as Jesus encourages me."

Paul writes, laying out 'ground rules' for growing and thriving (Jesus' training criterior). It's a whole training package with feedback, sorry no role-play, everything is for real. In the above passage, Paul writes they should:

- live life
- be worthy of being a citizen of God's kingdom
- be worthy of the gospel of Christ
- be steadfast in opposition
- see that they're privileged to both serve and suffer

Our response, as Paul shows, is to turn around every day, perhaps one step at a time, as we face and walk towards Jesus. In his own walk Paul's life is a daily struggle. He says, "To keep me from becoming conceited because of these surpassingly great revelations, there was given me a thorn in my flesh, a messenger of Satan, to torment me" (2Corinthians 12:7). Our lives may not be as thorny as his, but we each have a small thorn, or temptations, that require daily treatment.

Paul's 'ground rules' look something like this:

Live life
Our lives should be ones that reflect Jesus. "Be joyful in hope, patient in affliction, faithful in prayer. Share with God's people who are in need. Practice hospitality" (Romans 12:12-13). We are not to be grumpy Christians. Jesus is too wonderful not to share. Notice the reference to 'affliction'. That too is life. We are not without our own suffering. In knowing our own suffering, we know how to care for others suffering around us.

Be worthy of being a citizen of God's kingdom
Jesus beckons, calling out to us. So too does Satan, speaking softly. Who calls out the loudest surely wins. "Be very careful, then, how you live not as unwise but as wise, making the most of every opportunity, because the days are evil. Therefore do not be foolish, but understand what the Lord's will is" (Ephesians 5:15-17). We live as members of God's kingdom, aliens in a foreign land, waiting for repatriation. How are we filling our waiting time?

Be worthy of the gospel of Christ
"We preach Christ crucified: a stumbling block to Jews and foolishness to Gentiles" (1 Corinthians 1:23). Jesus' gospel just doesn't make sense – that's not how the world works, which is really the point. This world works on how much I can get, but Jesus' world works on how much I can give.

Be steadfast in opposition
For a while – 70, 80 years, or more (less for some), gravity fixes us. Our time and our lives are full – work, rest, hunger, pain, love, care, explore, guilt, passion – everyday, all day. Around us is a mocking world, full of suffering and pain, everyday, all day. For some their walk seems rather long and lonely. Ours is still the same walk, the same earth, the same time, but with one exception: Jesus. "I am the light of the world. Whoever follows me will never walk in darkness, but will have the light of life, Jesus Christ Son of God" (John 8:12).

See we are privileged to both serve and suffer
Personally, I'd prefer to be called to watch DVD's, or surf the net on my iPad, than serve or suffer. We're not built to serve and certainly not to suffer. Our own needs all too quickly become my only needs, excluding everything else. It's hard to serve. I'm not sure what to do or where I'm called. How do I tell? Suffering? No thanks, I've got a life.

Our daily steps, as Paul reminds us, are ones of growing more like Jesus. For some there is the total swing around. For the rest, it's a more gentle turn, but turn we do, as Jesus become more our central focus.

And what of Paul
He still inquires after the Philippians, asking them to write back to him. He misses them, as they gave him love and care when he was with them. They have just sent him a gift for which he thanks them dearly. He sends his greetings and reminds them of their journey with Jesus, one step, everyday. Steps are hard, till we see where they take us. Jesus wraps himself around us, just like an old and comfortable coat. When we first tried it on it might have felt a bit stiff and inflexible, now it's the most beautiful piece of clothing we own. Would you like one too? Jesus has lots to spare. It's in the shops – the line of clothing called 'His Way'.

Prayer

Forgive me Lord where I have wandered away from You. Parts of my life need Your hand to guide me more. Forgive me Father where my actions have hurt others, either through my own weakness or my selfish motives. Father, help me to make amends and show Your love and kindness wherever I have caused pain. Amen.

Memory verse

Psalm 18:6

In my distress I called to the LORD; I cried to my God for help. From his temple he heard my voice; my cry came before him, into his ears.

Action

Go and say "I'm sorry" to someone, where the sorry has become a bit overdue.

Day 44

The lamb or the vegetarian option

Reading: John 13:1-11

Jesus Washes His Disciples' Feet

¹ It was just before the Passover Feast. Jesus knew that the time had come for him to leave this world and go to the Father. Having loved his own who were in the world, he now showed them the full extent of his love. ² The evening meal was being served, and the devil had already prompted Judas Iscariot, son of Simon, to betray Jesus. ³ Jesus knew that the Father had put all things under his power, and that he had come from God and was returning to God; ⁴ so he got up from the meal, took off his outer clothing, and wrapped a towel around his waist. ⁵ After that, he poured water into a basin and began to wash his disciples' feet, drying them with the towel that was wrapped around him. ⁶ He came to Simon Peter, who said to him, "Lord, are you going to wash my feet?" ⁷ Jesus replied, "You do not realise now what I am doing, but later you will understand." ⁸ "No," said Peter, "you shall never wash my feet." Jesus answered, "Unless I wash you, you have no part with me." ⁹ "Then, Lord," Simon Peter replied, "not just my feet but my hands and my head as well!" ¹⁰ Jesus answered, "A person who has had a bath needs only to wash his feet; his whole body is clean. And you are clean, though not every one of you." ¹¹ For he knew who was going to betray him, and that was why he said not every one was clean.

Meditation

We all like a choice – the lamb or the vegetarian option? Usually, unless the restaurant is good, the veggie choice does look tempting. Peter had a choice: whether to have his feet washed by Jesus or not. But that's servant stuff, Jesus doesn't do that. He's the Kings of Kings, God's Son, the Emmanuel. Surely He doesn't do the foot washing thing. Yes He does, and He's very good at it (hot water and towel supplied).

The disciples still had a long way to go before they crouched, hiding upstairs in another Jerusalem room, waiting for Pentecost (the original one). They still had to see their Lord rejected, beaten, and mocked. They still had to see Him crucified, dead, and buried. We often forget as we read the Gospel accounts, the bewilderment they experienced. We know the ending – bit like the Titanic film (hits iceberg, sinks, good soundtrack). Jesus (crucified, dies, raised to life, redeems the world). Living in a post-resurrection society, we know of the salvation wrought by Jesus' death and resurrection. Not so the disciples. They were still learning about the servant Messiah and doing the foot washing thing.

Jesus is not only washing their feet, but showing them in this simple act, how they are to live their lives once He's resurrected. There is no other way for them to learn. They must experience service being given to them, in order to give service to others. This is the point that Jesus makes with Peter: "You must accept me as I am, your servant, so you too can serve. There is no other way. As a servant I must following the directions my Father gives me. I may not like them, but I am His servant, following His commands. I serve." This is where Jesus leads His disciples. He leads them into serving, by first serving them.

Each disciple has yet to learn their own personal understanding of service. There is little recorded of the disciples immediately after the Passover Supper. Thomas and Philip are seeking Jesus' guidance. We find Jesus asking Peter, James and John, the Sons of Zebedee, to keep watch as He prays, with Jesus returning to three sleeping disciples. We see Judas betraying Jesus, then hanging himself. Lastly, we see Peter denying Jesus three times. What of the others? They've fled, out into the Jerusalem night.

But the thing about servants is that they wait for the moment 'to be of service', when they can be useful. We see Jesus' disciples not hiding, more waiting. Following any amount of training comes the wait – a wait for action. Jesus knew how His disciples would react following His arrest. He knew they'd wait till it was all over, hoping to quietly leave Jerusalem, perhaps resume their old lives. He knew they'd eventually seek each other out for company and support.

Just as Jesus knew His disciples, He knows us too; how we're being moulded into His servants, in exactly the same way as His disciples were. We too need to experience service, to find that moment when we realise we cannot do it alone, that we need our feet washing. Jesus, if we let Him, washes our feet daily. When I pray, Lord hear me; when my friend hugs me, Lord hold me; when I say I'm sorry, Lord forgive me.

As we are washed by Jesus, we become part of what He's doing. He says to Peter, "Unless I wash you, you have no part with me." We take on the role of the waiting servant, just as the disciples did, waiting for their moment. We are 'servants in waiting'.

Jumping outside of today (because we know the story's ending – a risen Jesus and another sunk Titanic), we too need to receive His promise as He washed their feet, the gift of the Holy Spirit. "And I will ask the Father, and he will give you another Counsellor to be with you forever the Spirit of truth" (John 14:16-17). We are not alone. We have this promise.

Leaping to Acts this time, we see this gift given to frightened disciples as they huddle in another upper Jerusalem room. The Holy Spirit comes with power, lifting them to a place where they become unstoppable servants. Act 2 records tongues of fire resting on each disciple. We hear them speaking in the languages of the world as the

Spirit gives them power to share Jesus' message. Later, Peter and John begin their own healing ministry, right in Jerusalem. The city which so recently crucified Jesus, receives Jesus' servants who now know the ending, one of triumph and power.

The promise of Jesus is one given to all: "I am going to send you what my Father has promised ... you will be clothed with power from on high" (Luke 24:49). How the gift is given is unique to each – as we are each unique to God, so too are the gifts He gives.

> When he had finished washing their feet, he put on his clothes and returned to his place. "Do you understand what I have done for you?" he asked them. "You call me 'Teacher' and 'Lord,' and rightly so, for that is what I am. Now that I, your Lord and Teacher, have washed your feet, you also should wash one another's feet. I have set you an example that you should do as I have done for you. I tell you the truth, no servant is greater than his master, nor is a messenger greater than the one who sent him (John 13:12-16)

Jesus packs up His visual aid (washing bowl and all) and turns to His disciples checking they've got what's just happened. He shows how if we are going to be a servant and encourager we need to have our feet washed just like the disciples. If someone cares and serves us, will not we be challenged to serve and care as well?

One part of the feet washing story remains: "Now that you know these things, you will be blessed if you do them" (John 13:17). For Jesus, caring is an active occupation. Whatever that care might be, it's one of doing. If we care, John 13:17 applies.

Prayer

Father, thank you for the gift of Your Holy Spirit in my life. Empower me, and fill me afresh with the Holy Spirit, showing me how the Holy Spirit is working in my life. Guide me Lord throughout today in everything I'm doing, especially in my own unknown needs. Help me to be sensitive to the needs of those around me, considering them first, and how I may encourage them.

Memory verse

John 14:16-17

"And I will ask the Father, and he will give you another Counsellor to be with you forever – [17] the Spirit of truth."

Action

There may be people local to where you are, who are in need of feet washing. Alternatively, they may be in need of some other kind of practical help. How could you assist them?

Day 45

Jesus dies

Reading: Mark 15:33-41

The Death of Jesus

[33] At the sixth hour darkness came over the whole land until the ninth hour. [34] And at the ninth hour Jesus cried out in a loud voice, "Eloi, Eloi, lama sabachthani?" – which means, "My God, my God, why have you forsaken me?" [35] When some of those standing near heard this, they said, "Listen, he's calling Elijah." [36] One man ran, filled a sponge with wine vinegar, put it on a stick, and offered it to Jesus to drink. "Now leave him alone. Let's see if Elijah comes to take him down," he said. [37] With a loud cry, Jesus breathed his last. [38] The curtain of the temple was torn in two from top to bottom. [39] And when the centurion, who stood there in front of Jesus, heard his cry and saw how he died, he said, "Surely this man was the Son of God!" [40] Some women were watching from a distance. Among them were Mary Magdalene, Mary the mother of James the younger and of Joses, and Salome. [41] In Galilee these women had followed him and cared for his needs. Many other women who had come up with him to Jerusalem were also there.

Meditation

Arriving at a house just after someone's died, there's a noticeable stillness, the quietness of death, a pause inside the house. Outside the world busies itself; inside a life has passed. We look to where they lay, all too still now, gone, their life already a fading memory. One day, many days from now, we too will become a fading memory. We too will have lain there – we too have died. Jesus says of death, "I am the resurrection and the life. He who believes in me will live, even though he dies; and whoever lives and believes in me will never die. Do you believe this?" (John 11: 25-26). Do we? Sometimes, just occasionally, amongst the grief, we don't. The sadness is too much.

Arriving outside, we see the ambulance standing in the road, just stopped – not parked. Entering, the ambulance crew offer sympathy. Kind words, reassuring: "I'm sorry for your loss. Could you please just identify?" The litany of visitors to home deaths seems endless, all showering you with kindness and concern: a GP who did not know them, two police officers and their sergeant, another doctor. All are sorry for your loss. Eventually an undertaker does arrive – may we move them? – died at home, an autopsy, a formality.

And then it's you, just you alone. Well, never really alone. It's you and Jesus. It always is. Just you and Jesus right at the end in death. All the tears in the world are cried, with you and Jesus side by side. And then the visitors, in ones and twos, saying "Sorry for your loss." We may share some stories, moments precious to ourselves made public in their death. Love and care are shared as tears seem hard to cry.

With death come duties and choices strange. You leaf through the undertakers brochures finding latest designer coffins, the 'look' for this year, and then there's the choice of burial or cremation. These handles match, not those, they're brass. Is that OK? No it's not OK. I want them back, I miss them so. Why do we have to die? Please tell me that!

The music's played and now we're standing in that one last chapel to say goodbye. No closing curtains if you wish, just walk away. Goodbye, see you soon, in heaven. I love you, x.

One last job to round it off: a scattering of what's left. You get a box, all plastic red, with matching bag to go. The last remains – please don't be shocked, they're all too weighty things; a soft grey dust is the remains of those we loved so much. And afterwards, there's us, just us – no longer them, now only us (and Jesus).

So too with Jesus, formality and duties:

> Going to Pilate, [Joseph of Arimathea] asked for Jesus' body, and Pilate ordered that it be given to him. Joseph took the body, wrapped it in a clean linen cloth, and placed it in his own new tomb that he had cut out of the rock. He rolled a big stone in front of the entrance to the tomb and went away' (Matthew 27:58-60).

For most, death is private, quiet, unlike a public execution. Whether by firing squad, electric chair, a hangman's rope, a needle, the blunted axe or maybe fire, most who die in the name of justice die scared, alone, surrounded by justice bringing judgment of a kind. Jesus himself felt the fear of loneliness: "My God, my God, why have you forsaken me?" Compassion came offered on a stick with vinegar. That's all the care that this world offered to the Saviour of mankind as He died.

It seems strange, but the most recorded words in all our lives are our first and last. We crave for young children to utter something, reading meaning into every nuanced breath. And at our end, our dying breath, our words are recorded and broadcast to all. Our lifetimes worth of words lie unrecorded, ignored, so lost and forgotten. Our existence recalled in a few short phrases, our lives summed up, no more than 100 words to fit the obituary page. Tormented by His Father's rejection, and resolute in His destruction, Jesus cries out "It is finished!" (John 19:30). These were His last words to this world. His life was summed up by: "It is finished!" His earthly life and ministry done, His new heavenly ministry as Redeemer of the world had just begun.

And our own experience and thoughts of death – we all have them: hints of lights, gardens, angels, Jesus; we don't for certain know, although we sometimes wish we did. Hospice nurses waiting for death may see their patient's faces change from sullen despair to radiant bright just before they die. Others reaching out arms to embrace and smile with tears of joy as death envelops them.

Lastly, there is death shared only by the one who dies, alone and friendless to the world. There waiting for them is Jesus, asking of us the question of why they died alone. Did we not care, did we not know? We may not know, but if we did, perhaps we could, next time, care a little more.

What remains, and can only remain, in death is love. Like Joseph of Arimathea we may have duties: to bury, to choose a coffin (or box, as I call it) and some hymns, and then select a final resting site. In death our care too may begin. Perhaps like John caring for Jesus' mother Mary, we may find ourselves caring for a friend or relative. We are Jesus' hands and feet; there is no other who can minster to His people in need.

Emmanuel, given at Christmas a gift to the world, lies broken, disregarded, once loved, bleeding, forgotten to the world.

We can care for the dying of this world and the ones who remain in many ways. Death is not the end. As I love you, I will not lie to you – there is more yet to come.

Prayer

Father, I pray for those who have lost loved ones today. Comfort them in their loss and sadness. I pray for those who are dying with no one to care for them, for those whose deaths are unforeseen, for those waiting to die in hospices, and for those where death is not welcomed. Amen.

Memory verse

Psalm 138:7

Though I walk in the midst of trouble, you preserve my life; you stretch out your hand against the anger of my foes, with your right hand you save me.

Action

Go and sit with a friend and ask them what they think about death. Share with them your views and understandings of how death affects those left behind.

Day 46

A moment of your time please

Readings

1 John 4:7-12

God's Love and Ours

⁷ Dear friends, let us love one another, for love comes from God. Everyone who loves has been born of God and knows God. ⁸ Whoever does not love does not know God, because God is love. ⁹ This is how God showed his love among us: He sent his one and only Son into the world that we might live through him. ¹⁰ This is love: not that we loved God, but that he loved us and sent his Son as an atoning sacrifice for our sins. ¹¹ Dear friends, since God so loved us, we also ought to love one another. ¹² No one has ever seen God; but if we love one another, God lives in us and his love is made complete in us.

Matthew 3:3

Prepare a way for the Lord

³ This is he who was spoken of through the prophet Isaiah: "A voice of one calling in the desert, 'Prepare the way for the Lord, make straight paths for him.' "

Meditation

At the end of Lent there is a pause, a day when nothing seems to be happening. Jesus has died and not yet risen, and there is a day in between, separating His death from new life. Like all pauses it consists of three parts: beginnings, Jesus, and ourselves.

Beginnings

How's your Christmas planning coming on? It's never too early. Easter's upon us and soon the shops will be filled with Christmas fairy lights, decorations, and pre-Christmas sales. It gets earlier every year.

Preparation is the success key. The more we do, the better the event happens – the better the talk, the lesson, or the play goes. We would never dream of turning up without practising, without thinking through the possibilities. We wouldn't consider going ahead without having first considered all the available options and decided this is the one to pursue. The whole of Jesus' existence, His life and ministry, led Him to one and one point only, His death. He came for no other reason. He came to die, because sin, our sin, was in the world. The tiny baby lying sweetly in the manger seeks only death to rid our sin.

The way for Jesus was prepared long before His birth, as Matthew records, quoting Isaiah 40:3: "Prepare a way for the Lord" (Matthew 3:3). Plans, awful plans, were made for Jesus and his time on earth.

Imagine a heavenly 'Situations' or 'War Room'. The Father, Son, and Holy Spirit are there, working out how to remove sin from the world. All the options are evaluated, and it is decided Jesus is to be sent, except that to make it work He has to be rejected, suffer, and die to conquer sin. There was no other way. If there was, Jesus would have taken it.

Just like God, we sometimes have to make extremely painful or life changing decisions, ones we thought we'd never have to make. Dilemmas such as turning off a life support machine; not having that operation; rejecting our partners; turning away from family needs. As we consider these, we find it unbelievable that we're actually weighing up these options, considering doing one of them. It seems madness. Yet amongst the madness the decision is made, plans are prepared and set in motion, the unthinkable becomes acceptable. Was the unthinkable, that Jesus should die, part of God's plan when He created the world? Did He say, "Hey I know, let's make the earth; oh, and by the way, you'll have to die a really painful death. You OK with that?" Events require decisions and plans need preparation for accepting the unthinkable as the best option. It takes about 30 minutes to 2 hours to actually die when your life support machine is turned off; if the pain of turning it off was not enough, the dying person still registers blips on the monitor.

Because God thought the unthinkable, and decided, we can approach Him in the time of our unthinkable decisions. He knows our agonies, He's been tormented too. We not only have a Saviour in Jesus, we have a Comforter in God, who understands our agonised choices, the awful and painful ones. Once, long ago, God decided to turn off Jesus' life support machine, not a choice any father wants to make.

Then there was the new beginning, because there always is when you make the awful choice. God is there with His arms around us, silent with no more tears, "Mmmmmm, I feel you hurt too. See how it turns out though."

Jesus

Throughout Jesus' life, we see him fulfilling plans and prophecies about Himself. Each one links Him into the human time-line events, real occurrences at focal points. Jesus connects with humanity as no other individual has, before or since. As His life becomes entwined with humanity's, He enters into a relationship with us no other god has. He connects with us, allowing us to connect to Him. There are no barriers to Jesus, just those we ourselves may chose to create.

And the purpose of this connectivity as with any relationship is sharing. Most of our earthly relationships have moments of tension or disagreements. Our one with Jesus is no different. We may still disagree, feel upset, and not want to talk to him, but it's our barriers not His. Jesus provides the perfect relationship – He's always there, loving, caring, and nurturing. The problem is that that's not what we often want. Our wants demand a different relationship with Him, one where we are in control (as we know what's best for us).

Here we see a patient Jesus, waiting for the realisation of our needs, not our wants, to resurface. The connectivity we have with Jesus is one of love, as 1 John 4:7-12 portrays. With such love, occasionally there is a rather big gap in our connectivity, one we need Jesus to fill even more than perhaps He does at the moment.

As we experience Jesus in our lives He poses a challenge to us: can we respond by sharing the care that He gives: "Freely you have received, freely give" (Matthew 10:8).

Ourselves

Our understanding of ourselves and our own limitations often directs us to where we should consider improving ourselves. Self care from a worldly perspective is all about us, making sure 'we' function well. Jesus flips this on its head (as usual) into: 'Self' – examining our relationship with Jesus and His influence in our lives; and 'Care' – how we're responding to Jesus' ministrations in our lives. Hence 'Self Care' or, to put it another way, 'We care *because* we share' (nothing to do with Monsters Inc. who only scare)

As ~~scarers~~ carers, the world will make demands of us. There's only one way to survive in such an environment – with Jesus. We're promised "We can do all things through Him who gives us strength" (Philippians

4:13), which sometimes seems a little hard to see. Caring is not an easy option (and never will be), and although we have strength from God, sometimes it feels as though there's none at all. Lastly there's one more thing to consider: preparation.

Before we get to Easter Day and all that chocolate, there's John: "A voice of one calling in the desert" (Matthew 3:3) – the voice calling to all who would hear, "Prepare the way for the Lord, make straight paths for him." He calls us also to prepare for the Lord. He comes, but are you ready? During Lent we've prepared for Easter, the rising of Jesus from the dead, just as in Advent we've prepared for Jesus' birth. About twelve days after Christmas we have the Three (or however many you ascribed to) Wise Men (they made it quite quickly so they must have had a woman with them) arriving with gifts for Jesus: gold, frankincense, and myrrh – incredibly practical and useful, particularly if you're about to flee to foreign lands and need some portable finances. About fifty days after Easter, God sends His Holy Spirit as a gift to *us*, which is equally useful if you're about to embark on a life of caring for the people around you.

John still calls in the wilderness asking if we're prepared. Here Jesus comes, ready or not. We never are, as Easter just like Christmas comes far too quickly (whatever happened to those 40 days?)

Jesus has shared Himself with us, and God's sent as a present His Holy Spirit to help us out. As with all presents, we need to say thank you and unwrap it.

Prayer

Thank you Father for Your love in my life. Thank you for the many blessings you have given me. Show me how I may share with others what I have found in You. Father, also help me to see the areas of my life in which I need to reconsider and change, the areas where I need to grow and the areas where I too need help and assistance. Help me to be open to asking and accepting help from those around me. Amen.

Memory verse

John 3:16

"For God so loved the world that he gave his one and only Son, that whoever believes in him shall not perish but have eternal life."

Action

Go and ask someone you know well if they could help you with something, anything really – even asking's enough.

Day 47

Mmmmm, tea & chocolate

Readings

John 20:15-16

[15] "Woman, why are you crying?" Jesus asked her. "Who is it you are looking for?" Thinking he was the gardener, she said, "Sir, if you have carried him away, tell me where you have put him, and I will get him." [16] Jesus said to her, "Mary." She turned toward him and cried out in Aramaic, "Rabboni!" (which means Teacher).

Matthew 25:40

[40] "The King will reply, 'I tell you the truth, whatever you did for one of the least of these followers of mine, you did it for me.'"

Meditation

The early dawn tender in its light, seeps into our new day. A little chilly gentle breeze drifts past, the daylight blue grey tinting spots of rain or late dew dropping softly. It's not a quite place; birds warbling for their friends, competing with planes and cars for a voice; another day wakens, this one cooler than some Easters. There's no splintering rays of sun seeping past the clouds, only empty sunless sky. The dawn changes from night to early morning to proper day, as the sleeping world remembers its duties and stirs.

The morning's chilliness lasts as long as I have for my kettle to boil and then the warmth of the kitchen beckons. Yet if I walk not 1000 paces

I may find someone for whom the dawn remains all too cold and empty, where tea needs hunting down and breakfast is a hoped for delicacy.

Today, now, in the early morning comes Jesus, risen and ascended, into the new redeemed world. Mary turns and hears her name and knows He's risen. He is risen indeed; and soon we'll sing about our risen Lord and eat our longed for chocolate eggs. And 1000 paces from our singing is the woman who feels there is no hope.

It's colder now and the kettle's boiled, tea's arrived (with perhaps a little chocolate to keep me going). Another 1000 paces from me a man stands asking, a man in the early Jerusalem light: "When I needed some tea were you there? When I was cold and hungry were you there? When I was naked and alone, were you there?"

Were we?

I'd love to say I was, mostly because one day He's going to ask each and everyone: "Were you there when I needed you?"

Memory Verse

Philippians 4:14

It was very good of you to help me in my troubles.

Action

Put in your diary for 3 months time to ask yourself this question, "Have I made a difference in someone's life?" Then enjoy Easter Day, because He is Risen ☺

Notes

Notes

Notes

From the same publisher

TODAY

Daily Meditations for Abundant Living

ISBN 978-0-9562559-0-7

The Way of Heaven

Taking the Highest Path

ISBN 978-0-9562559-6-9

Available from Inspirational Faith at

inspirationalfaith.net

www.ingramcontent.com/pod-product-compliance
Lightning Source LLC
Chambersburg PA
CBHW070640160426
43194CB00009B/1519